I0037557

3 Keys to Maximize Profitability

Practical Strategies for Lasting Business Growth

A Guide to Boost Sales, Improve Margins, and Reduce Costs

CHARLIE VICTOR

Impisi™

Impisi™ Media LLC
Small Business Series

ISBN: 978-1-965722-09-1 (eBook)
ISBN: 978-1-965722-10-7 (Paperback)
ISBN: 978-1-965722-15-2 (Hardcover)

The case studies in this book are based on real-life experiences. To protect privacy, names, locations, and identifying details have been changed or omitted. Any resemblance to persons, businesses, or places beyond the intended examples is coincidental. The lessons and insights are genuine and provide practical guidance to readers on their entrepreneurial journey.

Book design by Ciska Venter.

First printing edition 2024.

Published by Impisi™ Media LLC in the United States of America.
5830 E 2ND ST, STE 7000, CASPER, WY 82609
+1 (307) 275 8745
www.impisimedia.com
Impisi™ is subject to a trademark application by Impisi Media LLC.

Contents

Table of Figures

There are multiple figures throughout the book. Below is the Table of Figures for easy reference.

Also by the Publisher

Small Business Series

Should You Start a Business or Not?
Business Entry: Starting vs Buying
3 Keys to Maximize Profitability

Smart Work-Life Series

Mastering Time for Productivity
The Wolf's Edge: Strategies for Intelligent Living
Reset with Intermittent Fasting

Click or scan the QR code to receive updates on new releases and book resources.

"The key to sustained profitability is to understand that profit is not the goal, but the result of serving others well" – Robin Sharma

Profit is the byproduct of value creation, not an end in itself. When we focus solely on profit, we miss the deeper purpose of business: to meet needs, solve problems, and improve lives. By serving others—clients, employees, and communities—we build trust and loyalty.

This creates lasting value, leading to sustainable success. True profitability arises not from chasing wealth but from the ripple effect of genuine service. It's the outcome of meaningful impact, not the motive.

Introduction

"Profit is not a four-letter word; it is the lifeblood of a healthy, sustainable business" – Howard Schultz

Purpose of the Book

The goal of this book is to provide small business owners and prospective entrepreneurs with clear, practical strategies to maximize profitability. Many businesses struggle with profitability not because they lack sales, but because they do not keep a balance between sales, gross profit, and expenses. This book simplifies that challenge, focusing on these three essential keys to profitability. By honing in on these areas, the book breaks down complex financial concepts into manageable steps, allowing readers to develop a deeper understanding of how to grow their business profitably.

This book isn't just about increasing sales or reducing costs. Instead, it takes a holistic approach to profitability, helping readers understand how each part of the income statement interacts. For instance, increasing sales might seem like a win, but if those sales come with thin margins or high operating costs, profitability could remain stagnant. The same goes for cutting expenses—cutting critical investments can hurt growth in the long run. Through this book, readers will learn how to improve sales without sacrificing gross profit and how to cut costs strategically without damaging the core of the business.

Written as part of the *Small Business Series*, this book serves both as a standalone resource and as a continuation of the journey for readers who have already explored the earlier titles. Each chapter builds on essential knowledge from earlier books, helping entrepreneurs navigate real-world business challenges. Whether you are at the start of your entrepreneurial journey or looking to improve an established business, this book gives you the tools to achieve profitability and sustainable success.

How to Use This Book

This book is designed to be a practical tool you can use to immediately improve your business's profitability. Each chapter focuses on one of the three essential keys: Sales, Gross Profit, and Expenses. Within each chapter, you'll find strategies, examples, and action steps that you can apply directly to your business. The structure is simple: learn the concept, understand how it applies, and take actionable steps to implement the strategies.

At the end of each chapter, there's a summary of the key points, followed by an action plan. These action plans are critical because they guide you in applying what you've just learned. Instead of just reading about business strategies, you'll be encouraged to put them into practice, allowing you to see real improvements in your business's bottom line. For example, after reading about how to increase sales, the action plan will help you identify practical steps to boost revenue without increasing costs unnecessarily.

The case studies in Chapter 7 provide real-world examples of how businesses have successfully applied the three keys to maximize profitability. By learning from these examples, you can adopt strategies that work in your specific context.

Lastly, remember that this book is not meant to be read just once. Keep it as a resource, revisiting chapters as your business grows and evolves. The principles in this book apply at every stage of the business life cycle, from startup to expansion. Use it as a guide to help you maintain focus on the three keys and continually drive profitability.

Why Profitability Matters

Profitability is more than just a financial goal; it's the cornerstone of any business's long-term success. At its core, profitability measures how well a company turns revenue into actual profit after accounting for all expenses. Without profitability, a business can't sustain itself, grow, or compete effectively in the marketplace. It's not just about making money—it's about building something that lasts.

The bigger picture of profitability extends beyond daily operations. Profit enables a business to invest in new opportunities, expand its market, and weather economic downturns. As business expert Jim Collins says, "Profitability is not the point of a business, but without it, the business cannot fulfill its purpose" (Collins, *Good to Great*). This quote highlights that while profitability isn't the only goal, it's a necessary condition for achieving any other goal a business might have, such as innovation, social impact, or growth.

A profitable business also has the ability to provide stability and security. According to the *Harvard Business Review*, "Profitability is the most reliable measure of a business's ability to stay competitive in the long run" (Harvard Business Review, 2020). In other words, profitability allows a business to continuously improve, innovate, and stay ahead of competitors. A business that is barely breaking even or, worse, losing money is vulnerable to market shifts, unexpected expenses, and cash flow issues.

Profitability is essential for long-term sustainability, and without it, even businesses with great products, services, or teams will struggle to survive. Over time, the lack of profitability erodes a business's ability to reinvest, leading to stagnation or failure. It is not enough to focus only on generating sales or building brand awareness—those efforts must result in profits that can fuel further growth. Without profitability, even the most promising ventures will find it difficult to sustain operations over the long term.

Our approach in this book is not just about "chasing money." We aim to help entrepreneurs build lasting value through a balanced focus on sales, gross profit, and expenses. Profitability is a byproduct of creating value for clients, managing costs efficiently, and making sound financial decisions. This book shows you how to do that in a way that benefits not only your bottom line but also the long-term sustainability of your business. It's about striking the right balance—one that ensures profitability without compromising the values or mission of your business.

The three keys outlined in this book—sales, gross profit, and expenses—are crucial to achieving and maintaining profitability. Sales drive revenue, but without proper margins, they won't lead to profit. Gross profit reveals how efficiently a business is producing its goods or services, and controlling expenses ensures that costs don't outpace revenue.

Together, these three factors create a framework that every business owner must understand to unlock profitability. They are interdependent, meaning that focusing too much on one while neglecting the others can lead to a lack of balance and, ultimately, a lack of profitability.

In conclusion, profitability is not plainly important—it is essential. It enables growth, ensures stability, and allows businesses to fulfill their broader purpose. Through the strategies in this book, you will learn how to harness the power of these three keys to build a business that is not only profitable but also sustainable for the long haul.

This book includes exclusive downloadable resources, detailed in the Appendices. To access them, visit www.impisimedia.com/resources. You'll need to register for a free account and enter the access code found in **Appendix A** to unlock the materials.

Chapter 1

The Income Statement in Perspective

"Profitability comes not from doing things, but from doing things right" – Philip Kotler

Overview

The income statement is a critical tool for understanding the financial health of any business. While there are several financial statements to consider, such as the balance sheet and cash flow statement, the income statement stands out. It provides a snapshot of your business's profitability over a specific period. For small business owners, this is a practical way to focus on the essentials that drive success.

One of the biggest mistakes entrepreneurs make is getting lost in corporate jargon and complex accounting terms. In reality, you don't need to be an accountant to use the income statement effectively. You just need to know where to look.

This chapter emphasizes a simplified approach, narrowing the focus to three key areas: Sales, Gross Profit, and Expenses. Mastering these three can unlock profitability.

We'll also introduce the importance of balance between these areas. Sales should grow, gross profit should increase, and expenses need to be managed wisely. This balanced approach ensures long-term profitability. In the following sections, we'll explore how focusing on these three essential elements can maximize your business's profitability.

The Income Statement's Role

An income statement is a vital tool that every business owner should understand and use. Much like a school report card summarizes a student's academic performance, the income statement does the same for your business.

It provides a clear summary of how well your company has performed over a specific period, helping you see if your business is making a profit or running at a loss. This report reflects the business's trading results for the period, offering insights into the areas that need attention.

The period covered by an income statement is always indicated in its title. For example, if you are reviewing your income statement for a specific month, it would be labeled as "Income Statement for the month ending 31 January 2024." If it is for the entire year, you might see "Income Statement for the year ending 31 December 2024." The period in the title allows you to pinpoint when the performance took place, making it easier to track trends and compare financial outcomes over different periods. This time-based approach gives you a focused view of your business's financial health at regular intervals.

The income statement is one of the three most essential accounting reports. Alongside the cash flow statement and balance sheet, it forms the foundation of your business's financial reporting. While the income statement gives you a picture of profitability, the cash flow statement reports on the actual cash entering and leaving the business. The balance sheet provides a snapshot of the company's financial position at a specific moment, detailing what the business owns (assets) and what it owes (liabilities).

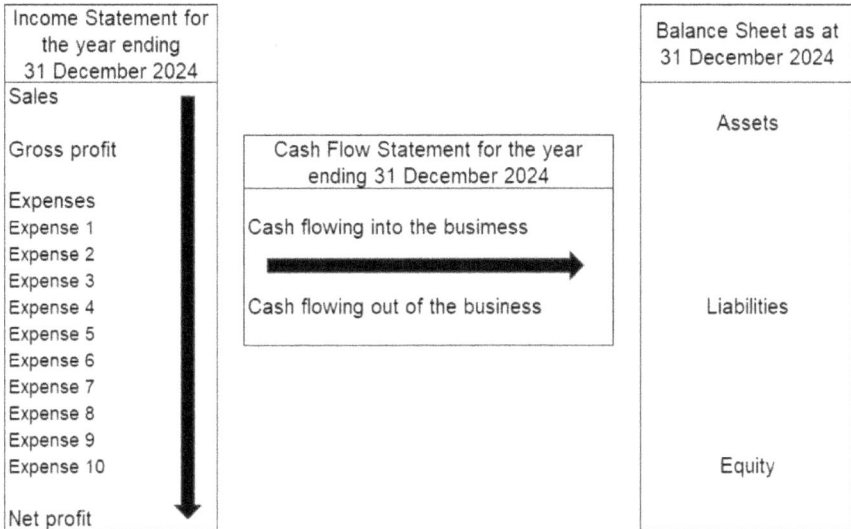

Figure 1.1: The three most important financial statements.

Note that, when using two or more financial statements together, such as the income statement and balance sheet, they should always have the same date in the heading to ensure that the same period and/or end of the period are being reviewed.

Together, these three financial statements provide a comprehensive view of the company's financial health. However, the income statement is the primary focus when analyzing profitability, as it directly connects to the core operations of the business.

The primary function of the income statement is to show the results of your business's trading activities. This report breaks down your revenue, costs, and resulting profit or loss over the period.

The top section of the income statement focuses on revenue, often called sales, which represents the money your business has earned from selling products or services. Directly below sales, you'll find the cost of goods sold (COGS), which reflects the expenses directly related to producing or delivering those products or services. When you subtract COGS from sales, you are left with gross profit, a key measure of your business's financial performance.

As you move down the income statement, you'll encounter a breakdown of operating expenses, which include rent, salaries, utilities, and other general business costs. Once all expenses are subtracted from gross profit, the result is your net profit or net loss, showing the final financial result for the period.

This figure at the bottom – the proverbial bottom line - is crucial as it highlights whether your business is operating profitably or not. By consistently reviewing and understanding your income statement, you can identify areas for improvement and make informed decisions that drive profitability.

The income statement holds the three essential keys to maximizing profitability: sales, gross profit, and expenses. These three areas are critical because they directly influence your bottom line. Increasing sales without a proportional increase in COGS boosts gross profit while controlling expenses ensures that more of your revenue turns into profit. This balance between sales growth, gross profit management, and expense control is at the heart of any successful business strategy.

Income Statement for the year ending 31 December 2024	
	Sales
less:	COGS
=	**Gross profit**
less:	**Expenses**
	Expense 1
	Expense 2
	Expense 3
	Expense 4
	Expense 5
	Expense 6
	Expense 7
	Expense 8
	Expense 9
	Expense 10
=	Net profit

Figure 1.2: Income Statement with the three essential keys

Throughout this book, we will consistently return to these three essential elements. Each chapter will give practical advice on how to improve sales, increase gross profit, and manage expenses efficiently.

Avoiding corporate jargon is vital. While large corporations may have complex financial systems and structures, small business owners need a straightforward, clear approach. That's why we'll use practical language and focus on simple, actionable steps that align with the realities of running a small business.

In summary, the income statement is more than just a financial report; it is a powerful tool for understanding and improving your business's profitability. By focusing on the three essential keys—sales, gross profit, and expenses—you can unlock greater financial success and sustain long-term growth. In the sections that follow, we will explore each of these areas in greater depth, providing you with the knowledge and tools needed to maximize your business's potential.

Simplicity for Success

When it comes to business planning, many entrepreneurs make the mistake of setting too many goals and objectives.[1] This overcomplication can lead to confusion, dilution of effort, and, ultimately, failure to achieve the most critical objectives.

Business expert Greg McKeown once said, "If you don't prioritize your life, someone else will." In his book *Essentialism: The Disciplined Pursuit of Less*, McKeown emphasizes the importance of focusing on fewer, more meaningful objectives to achieve success. This principle applies to financial management as well—focusing on a handful of core objectives will always yield better results than scattering efforts across too many areas.

The power of simplicity in planning cannot be overstated. When you limit your objectives to only a few critical areas, you allow for clearer focus and a greater chance of success. Small business owners, in particular, often wear multiple hats and are pulled in different directions. Simplifying your objectives can free up mental space and energy, enabling you to focus on what really matters. This doesn't mean that other areas of your business are not

---

1. **Goals** are broad, long-term aspirations that set the overall direction for a company or project. They are often qualitative and can be abstract. **Objectives** are specific, measurable, achievable, relevant, and time-bound (SMART) statements that outline the steps needed to achieve a goal. They are more concrete and quantifiable than goals.

important. Still, it does mean that by concentrating your efforts, you can achieve more significant results in the areas that directly affect profitability.

One of the main goals of this book is to help you simplify your financial objectives by concentrating on just three key areas of your income statement: Sales, Gross Profit, and Expenses. These three elements form the backbone of your business's financial health. By focusing on improving these areas, you'll naturally improve your overall net profit. The concept is simple, but its impact can be profound. Too often, businesses become lost in the weeds of trying to manage everything all at once. However, the key to long-term success is to focus on the few areas that truly drive profitability.

It's important to understand that net profit itself cannot be directly managed. Instead, it is the result of how well you manage your sales, gross profit, and expenses. Think of it like baking a cake. You can't manage the cake's quality directly—you can only manage the ingredients and the baking process. Similarly, you can't directly control net profit; instead, you manage the components thereof. By improving sales, optimizing gross profit, and reducing unnecessary expenses, net profit will improve naturally. This is the central concept of this book.

So, instead of setting broad and vague goals like "improving net profit," break it down into more specific objectives. For example, you might set objectives to increase sales by 10%, improve the gross profit margin by 2%, and reduce expenses by 5%. These objectives are clear, measurable, and directly related to improving the areas that contribute to net profit. By setting specific targets in these three key areas, you'll not only gain clarity on where to focus your efforts, but you'll also be more likely to see tangible improvements in your business's profitability.

This approach is so effective because it simplifies decision-making. Business owners often get caught up in trying to solve everything at once, leading to burnout and poor results. By focusing only on sales, gross profit, and expenses, you narrow your scope to what matters most. This makes it easier to track progress and adjust strategies as needed. When each of these three areas improves, the cumulative effect will naturally lead to a stronger bottom line.

In conclusion, the simplicity of focusing on these three key areas—sales, gross profit, and expenses—offers a straightforward yet powerful framework for achieving profitability. Rather than chasing the elusive goal of improving net profit directly, you should concentrate on improving the elements that lead to it. With this approach, your financial management becomes more focused, measurable, and actionable. You will see results not only in the form of improved profitability but also in your ability to manage your business more effectively.

Overview of the 3 Keys

In this section, we will provide a broad overview of the three key areas that will be the focus of this book: sales, gross profit, and expenses. Understanding these three elements and how they relate to each other is essential to unlocking profitability. While we will dive deeper into each of these in later chapters, this section gives you a foundational understanding to start with.

Sales

Sales represent the revenue your business generates by selling goods or services. Although "revenue" and "sales" are often used interchangeably, it's important to note that there can be a difference. Revenue encompasses all forms of income, including any additional earnings like interest or investment returns. For the sake of simplicity, we will use the term "sales" in this book to refer to all income earned directly from your core business activities. This helps to avoid confusion and keeps the focus on what truly matters for small business owners: the money earned through daily operations.

To further clarify, sales are typically measured in units, such as the number of products sold or the number of services provided. For example, if you own a coffee shop, your sales might be measured by the number of cups of coffee you sell each day. On the other hand, revenue is measured in monetary value. In the same coffee shop example, revenue would be the total dollar amount generated from those coffee sales. So, if you sold 100 cups of coffee at $3 each, your sales are 100 units, and your revenue is $300. Both terms are important, but for simplicity and practicality, we will generally refer to sales in this book.

Sales are a direct reflection of how well your business is performing in the marketplace. Every sale represents a client who has chosen your product or service over another. The more sales you make, the greater your income. However, increasing sales alone is not enough to guarantee profitability. Sales need to be accompanied by careful management of costs and expenses to ensure that they translate into actual profit. That is why sales are just one of the three keys to improving profitability, not the sole focus.

(i) In Appendix D: Supplemental Glossary, you'll find more detailed explanations of terms like "revenue" and other financial concepts that are not explored in depth in the main text. These terms may not be directly used in the book, but they are important for understanding the broader financial landscape.

Gross Profit

Gross profit is the profit your business earns from trading activities after deducting the cost of goods sold (COGS). This is essentially the money left over after paying for the direct costs associated with producing or delivering your product or service. For example, if you own a retail store, gross profit is what remains after deducting the cost of the items you sell. If you provide a service, it's the profit after paying for the direct labor and materials needed to provide that service.

Gross profit is a critical measure because it indicates how efficiently your business is producing and selling its goods or services.

It's important to note that gross profit only accounts for direct costs—those costs directly tied to production or service delivery. Other operating expenses like rent, utilities, and marketing costs are not included in gross profit. We'll cover those in the next section when we talk about expenses. For now, it's essential to understand that gross profit shows the profitability of your core business activities before accounting for other costs.

By focusing on gross profit as one of the three keys to profitability, you are ensuring that your business is operating efficiently and that your efforts to become more profitable translate into actual financial gains.

Expenses

Expenses are the costs your business incurs to operate. These costs can include rent, utilities, salaries, insurance, and other operational expenses that keep your business running. While gross profit focuses on the direct costs of producing goods or delivering services, expenses encompass everything else your business needs to function. In simple terms, these are the things that must be paid for to facilitate your trading activities.

Effective expense management is critical to maximizing profitability. While it's important to focus on improving sales and gross profit, cutting unnecessary or excessive expenses can have an immediate impact on your bottom line.

Later chapters will provide more detailed strategies for managing expenses effectively, but the key takeaway here is that controlling costs is just as important as generating revenue when it comes to boosting profitability.

In summary, sales, gross profit, and expenses are the three essential keys to maximizing your business's profitability. By focusing on improving each of these areas, you can drive meaningful financial improvements in your business. As we continue through this book, each chapter will explore these three areas in greater depth, providing practical strategies and actionable insights to help you succeed.

Chapter Recap

In this chapter, we explored the core components of the income statement and how they relate to profitability. The income statement provides a clear summary of your business's financial performance, highlighting sales, gross profit, and expenses. These three key areas are critical to understanding and improving profitability.

We emphasized the importance of focusing on simplicity for success. Concentrating your efforts on these three essential areas can effectively manage your business's financial health. It is crucial to remember that net profit cannot be managed directly; instead, it is the result of how well you manage sales, gross profit, and expenses.

Through this straightforward approach, business owners can gain better control over their financial outcomes, leading to long-term profitability and sustainability. The upcoming chapters will discuss each key area in more depth, with practical strategies for maximizing their business's success.

Chapter 2
Unlocking Sales Growth

"Profit in business comes from repeat clients, clients that boast about your project or service, and that bring friends with them" – W Edwards Deming

Overview

Sales growth is the lifeblood of profitability. This chapter will explore how increasing sales directly impacts your business's bottom line. Sales aren't just about pushing products; they're about understanding clients versus clients. In many successful businesses, the term "client" reflects a deeper relationship. Treating someone as a client builds long-term loyalty, creating a strong business culture where trust and value are essential.

Marketing plays a central role in driving sales. Often misunderstood as mere advertising, marketing is a broad concept that covers everything from identifying your target market to creating strategies that make your business stand out. We'll look at how branding can shape perception and increase sales, no matter the size of your business. Strong branding communicates value and builds trust with clients, which, in turn, fuels growth.

To sell effectively, it's crucial to know your target market. This involves segmenting clients into groups based on specific traits. By understanding who your ideal client is, you can tailor your marketing and sales efforts, leading to higher success rates.

The next step is finding the best routes to market. Whether through partnerships or direct-to-consumer strategies, knowing how to reach clients is essential. We will also dive into the various sales channels you can use, from online marketplaces to offline storefronts, and explore pricing strategies that balance client acquisition with retention.

Clients vs Customers

The terms "clients" and "customers" are often used interchangeably, though they can carry distinct meanings depending on the country, industry, or even individual business preferences. In some sectors, particularly retail, "customer" is the more common term. In contrast, industries such as law, finance, and consulting prefer "client," which implies a deeper, ongoing relationship. Both terms refer to someone who buys goods or services, but the nuance between them is important.

A "customer" is generally defined as someone who buys a product or service, often in a one-time or transactional manner. Think of a customer at a grocery store. There may not be a lasting relationship beyond the exchange of money for goods. A "client," however, is someone who seeks ongoing services or advice, such as a business receiving consulting services. This relationship is typically more professional and strategic.

Incorporating the term "client" into your business culture can signal a long-term, value-driven relationship. It reflects an ongoing commitment to the individual's success or satisfaction rather than just focusing on a single sale. A client relationship suggests a partnership where the business invests in understanding and addressing the client's evolving needs. This can lead to greater loyalty, higher lifetime value, and increased referrals.

By fostering a culture that treats buyers as clients, businesses can create a more personalized, strategic approach to communication. This subtle shift can elevate your brand, creating stronger, more meaningful connections with your target market.

Understanding Sales Growth

Sales growth refers to the increase in revenue that a business generates over a specific period. It is one of the most fundamental indicators of a company's success. Growth can be measured by comparing sales figures from one period to another, such as month-on-month or year-on-year. It is often expressed as a percentage and provides a clear picture of whether a business is expanding or stagnating.

Sales growth is typically the result of several factors, including increased demand for products or services, effective marketing campaigns, or the introduction of new offerings. Measuring growth allows businesses to assess the effectiveness of their sales and marketing strategies and make informed decisions about future actions. For example, if a business sees a 10% increase in sales over the previous quarter, it may show that recent efforts to target a new market segment have been successful. Conversely, if sales stay flat, it signals the need for a change in approach.

Sales growth is critical for profitability because it directly impacts a company's revenue. Increased sales provide businesses with more income, which can be reinvested in operations, expansion, or marketing efforts. Furthermore, as sales grow, businesses often benefit from economies of scale.

Sustained sales growth also plays a crucial role in attracting investors. Whether through equity investment or loans, investors typically look for businesses that demonstrate consistent growth.

A company with stagnant or declining sales may find it difficult to secure external funding, while a company with a track record of growth will be seen as a lower-risk investment. Additionally, sustained sales growth can boost a company's valuation, making it more attractive for acquisition or expansion opportunities.

In conclusion, sales growth is a vital part of any business's long-term success. It not only drives revenue but also helps lower costs and attract investment. For these reasons, understanding and managing sales growth is crucial for maintaining and increasing profitability. Every business owner must keep an eye on this key metric to ensure their company's future health and expansion.

Marketing in Perspective

Marketing is often misunderstood as simply advertising or sales tactics. However, it's a much broader concept that encompasses a wide range of activities aimed at promoting and selling products or services. The word "marketing" is often used as a catch-all term for anything related to achieving sales, but it's essential to understand the full scope.

Marketing involves everything from branding to pricing strategies, from market research to client relationship management (CRM). To unlock sales growth, one must grasp the key components of marketing.

To start, it's important to distinguish between a *marketing strategy* and a *marketing plan*, as these terms are often confused. A marketing strategy is like the architectural blueprint of a house. It defines the overall design, layout, and purpose. Your strategy lays out the big-picture approach for positioning your business in the market, determining your target audience, and defining your unique selling proposition (USP). It outlines the company's long-term goals and competitive positioning.

On the other hand, a marketing plan is akin to the construction plan for that house. It specifies the materials, timelines, and steps needed to bring the blueprint to life. The plan is tactical, detailing the specific actions, tools, and campaigns that will be used to achieve the goals set out in the marketing strategy. It includes things like advertising campaigns, pricing structures, promotional activities, and CRM systems.

With that distinction clear, what exactly does marketing entail? At its core, marketing is the process of identifying client needs and finding the most effective way to meet them. Marketing connects products or services with a target audience by communicating value and positioning the business favorably in the marketplace. The key is that marketing is not just about getting the sale but about building a lasting relationship with the client.

Here are some of the essential elements that fall under the marketing umbrella:

Branding – Branding involves creating a distinct identity for your business, including your logo, tagline, and overall image. A strong brand helps differentiate your business from competitors, communicates your values, and builds trust with your clients.

Market Positioning – Market positioning refers to the place your product or service holds in the minds of your target audience compared to your competitors. This positioning is influenced by your pricing, quality, and how your brand is perceived. Proper positioning helps ensure that your offerings resonate with your audience and stand out in a crowded market.

Market Research involves gathering data about your target audience, competitors, and industry trends. It helps you understand client preferences, behaviors, and unmet needs, allowing you to tailor your marketing efforts effectively.

Advertising and Promotion – Advertising is the paid promotion of your products or services through various channels such as online ads, TV, print, and social media. Promotion encompasses a broader range of tactics aimed at increasing awareness and sales, including exclusive offers, discounts, and events.

Pricing Strategy – Pricing is a crucial part of marketing that affects both profitability and market positioning. The right pricing strategy considers production costs, competitors' prices, and the perceived value of the product or service. Pricing also influences how your business is positioned in the market—whether as a premium or budget-friendly option.

Public Relations (PR) focuses on managing your business's reputation and building a positive image. Effective PR can enhance credibility, create goodwill, and foster strong relationships with stakeholders, including clients, investors, and the media.

Client Relationship Management (CRM) is about maintaining and managing interactions with clients. A sound CRM system helps businesses track leads, manage client interactions, and build long-term relationships. CRM is critical for client retention, which can often be more cost-effective than constantly acquiring new clients.

Sales Channels – Sales channels refer to the avenues through which you sell your product or service. These could be online platforms, physical stores, or third-party distributors. Identifying the proper sales channels is vital to reach your target audience effectively.

Routes to Market – This refers to the broader strategies for how your products or services reach the market. It includes direct sales, partnerships, or licensing deals, each of which has its own advantages and challenges.

Client Retention – Retaining clients often costs less than acquiring new ones. A strong focus on client retention—through excellent service, loyalty programs, or continuous engagement—leads to long-term profitability.

Content Marketing – This involves creating valuable content (blogs, videos, social media posts) to engage your audience. Content marketing builds trust, enhances brand authority, and draws clients to your website or store.

Digital Marketing – In today's digital world, online presence is critical. Digital marketing covers everything from search engine optimization (SEO) to social media, email campaigns, and online advertising. It allows you to target clients more effectively and measure campaign performance in real time.

Public Relations (PR) – Managing your business's public image and reputation, particularly through media relations and communication. PR plays a key role in shaping how the public and clients perceive your brand.

These various activities make up the holistic view of marketing, each contributing to driving sales and building client relationships.

In the remainder of this chapter, we will explore six of marketing's more prominent aspects: branding, target market segmentation, routes to market, sales channels, pricing strategies, and client retention. Understanding these key components will help you design a focused marketing approach that drives sales growth and positions your business for long-term success.

Branding

Branding is a multifaceted concept that goes far beyond a logo or a tagline. At its core, branding is your business's identity—how your company is perceived by others and what it stands for. It represents the values, personality, and unique traits that make your business different from competitors.

A brand is the promise you make to your clients about the quality and experience they can expect from you. This perception is built over time through consistent messaging, visual elements, customer interactions, and the overall experience clients have with your business.

For small businesses and large corporations alike, branding is essential, but the approach can differ significantly. Large corporations typically have massive budgets to invest in sophisticated branding strategies that involve market research, advertising campaigns, and highly polished visuals. They focus on reinforcing their brand identity on a global scale, often tailoring their message to different regions and customer segments.

Small businesses, on the other hand, often have limited resources and need to be more focused and efficient with their branding efforts. While they may not have the same reach as a corporation, their branding is no less important. In fact, for small businesses, branding can be the key to differentiating themselves in crowded markets and building loyal client relationships. A well-defined brand helps smaller businesses convey their unique selling proposition (USP), build trust, and attract the right clients.

Strong branding is critical even for small businesses. It helps prove credibility, increases visibility, and fosters trust among potential clients. Consistency in branding—whether through visuals, messaging, or customer experience—ensures that your business stays memorable and relatable. For businesses operating in highly competitive environments, branding is often what makes the difference between success and failure. A small business with a strong brand will find it easier to build lasting relationships and stand out from the competition.

Branding is a vast topic in its own right, but there are a few key aspects every business owner should focus on. These elements play a significant role in shaping your brand's identity and determining how effectively it resonates with your target audience.

Brand Identity

Brand identity includes all the visible elements of your brand, such as your logo, colors, fonts, and design choices. It's the visual representation of your brand that clients will immediately recognize. Having a consistent brand identity across all platforms (website, social media, emails) builds familiarity and trust. For example, think about iconic brands like Coca-Cola or Apple. Their logos and colors are instantly recognizable and evoke certain emotions. Small businesses, while not on the same scale, can still create a distinct brand identity that makes a memorable impression.

Brand Voice and Messaging

Your brand voice is the tone you use when communicating with clients. It reflects your company's personality and values. Whether your voice is formal and authoritative or casual and friendly, it should remain consistent across all client interactions. This consistency helps clients connect with your brand on a deeper level, fostering loyalty and trust. The message you convey through your brand voice should be clear, concise, and tailored to resonate with your ideal client.

Brand Promise

A brand promise is the commitment you make to your clients. It tells them what they can expect from your products or services every time they interact with your business. A strong brand promise is essential for building trust and reliability. Whether it's delivering exceptional customer service or offering innovative solutions, your brand promise should be clear and consistently delivered.

Brand Strategy

Every interaction a client has with your business contributes to your overall brand. From the first point of contact to post-purchase support, providing a seamless and positive customer experience strengthens your brand's reputation. Clients who align their experience with your brand's promise are more likely to become repeat buyers and recommend your business to others.

To help refine your brand strategy, consider asking yourself the following five key questions:

1. Who is your ideal client?

Knowing your ideal client allows you to tailor your branding efforts to resonate with the right audience. This is the person who not only needs what you offer but is also aligned with your values and vision. Defining your audience helps ensure that your message speaks directly to those who are most likely to engage with your brand.

2. What is your ideal client's perception of your business?

Understanding how your clients perceive your brand is essential for shaping your strategy. Gathering feedback through surveys, informal conversations, or direct interviews can provide valuable insights. Since not all clients will voluntarily share their opinions, you may need to ask directly to gain the insights necessary to adjust your branding.

3. What is your clear and concise message?

Your brand needs to stand out in a crowded marketplace. A clear, concise message allows you to capture attention quickly. Imagine meeting your ideal client at a networking event. How would you explain what you do in 30 seconds? This "elevator pitch" should be applied consistently across all client interactions to reinforce your brand's message.

4. Do you have a proven process that converts attention into sales?

Once you've captured the attention of your ideal client, you need a strategy to guide them through the customer journey. Whether through email campaigns, targeted content, or personalized offers, having a system in place that nurtures leads will result in more conversions and stronger client relationships.

5. Are you tracking results and refining your strategy?

Many businesses do not monitor the effectiveness of their branding efforts. Implementing tracking measures such as dedicated landing pages or client surveys helps gather data on what's working and what isn't. This data allows you to refine your branding strategy, ensuring it evolves with your clients' needs and perceptions.

(i) In Appendix B: Resources, you will find a downloadable copy of the five questions and further guidance in Word format: Brand Strategy and Positioning template.

As entrepreneur Ellen Sedge discusses in *The Wolf's Edge - Strategies for Intelligent Living*, a clear message is vital for a cohesive business culture. She suggests developing a "hymn sheet" to ensure that everyone in the business is aligned with the brand's core message. This document pays specific attention to the so-called elevator pitch.

(i) Please refer to Appendix B: Resources, for a link to the hymn sheet template.

In essence, strong branding ensures that your business speaks with one voice, providing clarity and trust for your clients.

Target Market and Client Segmentation

Understanding and identifying the right clients is a cornerstone of driving sales. Knowing exactly who you're targeting allows you to tailor your marketing, products, and services to meet their needs more precisely, resulting in higher engagement, loyalty, and sales. This starts with defining your *target market*—the specific group of people or businesses most likely to benefit from and purchase your offerings.

Target Market

A *target market* is essentially the ideal audience for your products or services. It's defined by several factors, such as demographics, behaviors, and needs. For example, a high-end fitness brand may target affluent, health-conscious adults between 30 and 50 who are interested in premium wellness experiences. Another example could be a small business offering tax services that target freelancers and gig workers in urban areas, helping them navigate complex tax requirements.

Identifying the correct target market is crucial because it allows you to focus your resources on clients who are most likely to buy from you. When you know who your ideal clients are, you can craft messages, select marketing channels, and design offers that resonate with them. Conversely, not identifying the correct target market can lead to wasted time and money. Marketing to the wrong audience often results in low engagement, poor conversion rates, and wasted marketing expenses. Imagine a luxury car brand trying to market to college students; even if they reach a large audience, few are likely to convert to sales. Precision in identifying your target market helps avoid this and ensures every marketing dollar is spent wisely.

Client Segmentation

Once the target market is identified, the next step is *client segmentation*. Client segmentation is the process of dividing your target market into smaller, more manageable groups based on shared characteristics or needs. This allows for more targeted marketing efforts, as each segment can be approached with tailored messages and strategies that align with their specific preferences.

The process of client segmentation typically involves several steps. First, you gather data on your target audience, including demographics, behavior, buying patterns, and psychographics. This data is then analyzed to find meaningful patterns and group clients with similar traits or needs together. Common segmentation criteria include age, location, income, buying habits, and lifestyle. For example, a skincare brand may segment its audience based on skin type (such as oily, dry, or sensitive) and then create specialized marketing messages and product recommendations for each segment.

Client segmentation is crucial because it allows businesses to personalize their marketing. People respond more positively to messages that feel relevant to them. With segmented marketing, you can address the unique needs of each group, which can lead to higher conversion rates and stronger brand loyalty. Segmentation also enables businesses to allocate resources more effectively, focusing on the segments with the highest potential for return on investment.

Client Segmentation Aligned with Branding

It's important to note that while client segmentation aligns with branding exercises, it is not the same as answering the five branding questions (e.g., defining the ideal client and developing a clear message). Branding focuses more on shaping your business's overall image, voice, and promise to create a cohesive identity. Client segmentation, however, is more about operationalizing that brand by finding and targeting the most relevant groups within the target market. They overlap, as segmentation provides the structure through which the brand message reaches different parts of the audience, but branding establishes the foundation and tone that every segment will experience.

Accurate identification of your target market and strategic segmentation of that market can drive sales significantly. By focusing on the right audience and addressing their specific needs, businesses create a more compelling value proposition. Marketing becomes more efficient, and clients are more likely to feel a strong connection to the brand. Ultimately, this leads to increased sales, greater customer loyalty, and a more sustainable business.

Routes to Market

Routes to market refer to the various strategic pathways a business uses to get its products or services to the intended audience. They encompass the broad approach a company takes to reach clients, including the processes and partnerships that support product delivery. Unlike sales channels, which are specific places or platforms where sales occur, routes to market are high-level strategies guiding how a product gets to the client. Routes to market include methods like direct-to-consumer sales, using distributors, licensing, and joint ventures. Each route has distinct advantages, costs, and potential challenges, making the right choice crucial for business success.

For small businesses, identifying and establishing effective routes to market is just as important as it is for larger corporations. Small businesses often operate on limited budgets, so selecting the most effective route can ensure that resources are focused where they'll yield the highest return. A well-chosen route to market helps small businesses reach their target audience more efficiently, bypassing some of the costly or complex distribution structures that larger businesses can afford. By focusing on the most direct or accessible paths to their audience, small businesses can achieve higher visibility, reduce overhead costs, and build a solid client base.

Routes to market also closely align with branding and client segmentation. An established brand identity will influence which routes are most appropriate. For instance, a luxury brand might avoid routes that dilute its premium positioning, like discount partnerships. Additionally, the process of client segmentation clarifies who the business wants to reach and their preferred buying methods, which directly affects route selection. A business with segmented clients who prefer digital interactions, for example, might prioritize e-commerce or partnerships with online retailers as its primary route to market.

Figuring out the best route to market is a strategic exercise that involves several steps. First, businesses need to understand their ideal client's purchasing behavior and preferred interaction channels. This involves examining whether clients prefer direct purchases, value-added resellers, or exclusive distribution arrangements. Researching competitors' routes to market can also provide insight into effective strategies and potential market gaps. Next, aligning the chosen route with the brand identity is crucial to ensure that the route reinforces, rather than contradicts, the brand image. Additionally, testing and iterating on routes can be valuable, especially for small businesses. Piloting a particular route, such as a pop-up shop or an online store, allows businesses to gather client feedback and make adjustments before committing to a larger rollout.

For instance, consider a small organic skincare brand that focuses on eco-friendly products. To reach clients effectively, they might choose a direct-to-consumer approach via an online store, allowing them to control the client experience from start to finish. They could also partner with select eco-conscious retailers to reach clients who value sustainable shopping. By choosing these routes, the brand ensures that its products are available where environmentally conscious consumers shop, aligning with its branding and segmented target audience.

Getting routes to market right can significantly drive sales by ensuring that products or services reach clients in ways that resonate with their preferences. When a business understands where its clients are most likely to shop or engage, it can position its offerings strategically to maximize visibility and accessibility. For example, a boutique coffee roaster might choose direct-to-consumer sales as its main route, supported by a subscription model that appeals to clients who value convenience and exclusivity. The roaster could then expand its reach by selling through specialty grocery stores that cater to discerning coffee lovers. This route selection not only aligns with the brand's identity but also meets the specific needs of its segmented clients, thereby increasing sales.

In summary, routes to market form a critical part of any sales strategy by establishing clear pathways to connect products with clients. For small businesses, these routes must be carefully chosen to align with branding, reach the right segments, and maximize limited resources. When aligned with a strong brand and a well-defined target audience, the correct route to market can drive significant sales growth.

Sales Channels: Their Role and Potential

A sales channel is the pathway through which a business sells its products or services to its clients. Essentially, sales channels are the tactical means by which goods or services travel from the seller to the buyer, facilitating the purchase process and driving revenue. Sales channels focus on specific avenues of distribution—direct, indirect, or digital—and impact how a company can effectively reach its target audience.

While similar in function, sales channels differ from routes to market. The route to market represents the overall strategy for reaching potential clients, while sales channels are the specific roads taken to get there. Think of it as planning a road trip: the route to market is the broader travel itinerary, while sales channels are the individual roads, highways, or shortcuts chosen to reach each destination.

Examples of Sales Channels

Direct Sales – Selling directly to clients without third-party involvement. Direct sales may include company-owned websites, physical storefronts, and personalized sales interactions.

Retail Sales – Working with third-party retailers, from large retail chains to small boutiques, helps get products into the hands of consumers through an established storefront.

Wholesale – Selling in bulk to distributors, who then sell to retailers or other vendors. Wholesale channels increase a company's market reach by moving larger volumes.

Online Marketplaces – Platforms like Amazon, Etsy, and eBay allow companies to reach broad audiences, providing a ready-to-use marketplace with established client bases.

Social Media Sales – Platforms like Facebook, Instagram, and TikTok offer in-app buying features, making it easy for clients to buy directly through social media.

Affiliate Sales – Partnering with affiliates such as influencers or bloggers who promote the product in exchange for a commission on sales. This channel leverages the established trust affiliates have with their followers.

Mobile Apps – Companies can create exclusive sales channels within their apps, offering personalized shopping experiences and client loyalty programs.

Direct Mail and Telemarketing – These traditional sales channels are particularly effective for businesses targeting older or niche demographics. Direct mail can include catalogs or targeted promotions, while telemarketing engages clients through personalized calls.

Distribution Partnerships – Working with a large distribution partner, such as a national grocery chain for a food product, allows small businesses to use existing networks to reach new clients.

Pop-Up Shops and Events – Temporary storefronts or event booths create unique, face-to-face interactions, help businesses build local communities, and engage clients directly.

B2B Sales – Selling directly to other businesses, often for products that companies need to operate. B2B sales are typically large-volume transactions involving long-term contracts.

Examples of Sales Channel Combinations and Changes

A small business that produces organic honey uses an innovative combination of sales channels to increase market reach. They initially sold through their website but soon expanded to online marketplaces like Etsy to reach a broader audience. To build a local presence, they began offering products at farmer's markets and pop-up shops at health-focused events. This combination allowed them to tap into online sales while establishing a community presence, effectively reaching both digital and in-person shoppers.

In another example, a small software company initially relied on direct sales through its website. To scale, they researched additional channels and decided to list their software on Amazon and integrate LinkedIn sales to target B2B clients. By adding these new channels, they reached clients they couldn't reach previously. Within a few months, the company saw a significant increase in sales. The change in sales channels was instrumental in expanding their reach and increasing revenue.

Pricing Strategies

A pricing strategy is a planned approach to setting and adjusting prices to achieve specific business goals. It determines how much a business charges for its products or services and directly affects sales volume and gross profit. While pricing strategies are crucial to a business's overall profitability, this discussion will focus on how these strategies drive sales growth specifically.

Pricing is a crucial lever in driving sales. The price of a product influences how potential clients perceive its value and affects their purchasing decisions. For many clients, price is a determining factor, and finding the right balance between affordability and profitability is essential. Setting prices too high can limit accessibility and deter clients, while prices that are too low can create a perception of low quality or unsustainable value. The challenge lies in finding the optimal price that appeals to the target market, encourages sales, and aligns with the brand's positioning.

Small businesses have a variety of pricing strategies at their disposal. Some popular approaches include cost-plus pricing, where a fixed margin is added to the cost of goods; value-based pricing, which sets prices based on perceived client value; and penetration pricing, where an initially low price is used to capture market share. There's also premium pricing, which positions products as high-end or exclusive, and competitive pricing, which benchmarks prices against competitors. Each strategy has unique advantages and is suited to different business goals and client segments.

Although many businesses resort to lowering prices to boost sales, this tactic isn't always the best option. A lower price might increase the quantity sold, but it can also reduce revenue if the drop in price outweighs the increase in volume. For instance, if a business reduces the price of a product from $100 to $80 to boost sales, it would need to sell significantly more units to maintain the same level of revenue.

Additionally, lower prices can devalue a brand by creating the perception of lower quality. In some cases, clients may view a higher price as a sign of superior quality or exclusivity. Thus, lowering prices can sometimes lead to higher sales volumes but reduced revenue or an altered brand image.

Examples How Pricing Strategies Can Affect Sales

Example 1: A Successful Pricing Strategy

A small bakery specializing in artisanal pastries decided to adopt a value-based pricing strategy. After researching local competition and understanding client preferences, the bakery set its prices slightly above the market average, emphasizing the premium ingredients and craftsmanship involved.

The owner noticed that many clients valued the uniqueness and quality of the pastries and were willing to pay more for an exclusive, handmade product. As a result, sales increased, and the bakery attracted a loyal client base that appreciated the higher quality.

By aligning price with perceived value, the bakery drove sales growth without sacrificing revenue or brand image.

Example 2: A Pricing Strategy That Didn't Work

In another case, a local gym wanted to increase membership sales by adopting a penetration pricing strategy. They lowered their monthly membership fee significantly, hoping to attract more clients quickly. While they gained a few new members, the overall sales volume did not increase as expected. Most of the existing clients had already chosen the gym based on its facilities and reputation, and the price reduction did not appeal to their desire for quality services. Additionally, some potential clients viewed the lower price as a sign that the gym might lack advanced amenities or be in financial trouble. In this case, the pricing change didn't boost sales, and the gym ultimately returned to its original pricing, recognizing that its client base valued quality over low prices.

In conclusion, pricing strategies play an essential role in driving sales and achieving growth. Selecting the right strategy depends on the business's target market, brand positioning, and client expectations. Simply lowering prices may seem like a quick solution, but it can have unintended consequences on revenue, brand image, and client perceptions. Instead, small businesses can benefit from exploring various pricing strategies that align with client needs, ultimately leading to a sustainable and profitable sales increase.

Client Retention vs. Acquisition

Client retention and client acquisition are two distinct but complementary aspects of growing a business. Both strategies involve different approaches and goals but aim to enhance sales and profitability. *Client acquisition* refers to attracting new clients to the business, requiring outreach efforts like advertising, promotions, and marketing campaigns designed to capture the attention of potential clients. *Client retention*, on the other hand, focuses on keeping existing clients engaged, satisfied, and loyal, which encourages repeat purchases and long-term relationships.

While both client retention and acquisition are essential, they serve different purposes within the overall sales strategy. Acquisition brings fresh revenue and widens the client base, introducing the brand to new audiences. Retention, however, emphasizes building relationships with current clients, which can result in lower marketing costs, as keeping an existing client typically costs less than acquiring a new one. Retention strategies involve maintaining client satisfaction, offering added value, and fostering loyalty. In short, acquisition grows the client base, while retention maximizes value from existing relationships.

Focusing on client retention can be especially advantageous for small businesses. Retaining clients not only reduces acquisition costs but also boosts profitability by increasing the lifetime value of each client. Clients who feel valued and appreciated are more likely to make repeat purchases, refer others, and give positive reviews, all of which contribute to sustained growth. For a small business, establishing a loyal client base can create a steady revenue stream that helps weather economic fluctuations and minimizes the need for extensive advertising campaigns.

> "Do what you do so well that they will want to see it again and bring their friends" - Walt Disney

Here are some practical ways small businesses can focus on client retention:

Excellent Customer Service

Providing outstanding customer service is one of the most effective ways to retain clients. When clients feel listened to and supported, they are more likely to return. Small businesses can achieve this by training their staff to be responsive, attentive, and empathetic. Whether through phone, email, or in-person interactions, consistently positive client service experiences build trust and loyalty. For example, if a client has an issue with a product, promptly addressing their concern and offering a solution shows them that the business values their satisfaction.

Personalization

Personalized experiences make clients feel valued and understood. Small businesses have an advantage over larger corporations in this regard, as they can easily offer tailored services or communications. Personalized emails, birthday discounts, and product recommendations based on earlier purchases all enhance the client experience. Small touches like these prove that the business remembers and appreciates the client, which strengthens the relationship.

Loyalty Programs

Loyalty programs incentivize clients to continue buying from the business. These programs can be as simple as a punch card for a free item after a certain number of purchases or as sophisticated as a points-based system for discounts. Small businesses can also offer exclusive deals or early access to new products for loyal clients. Such rewards encourage clients to stay engaged and feel recognized for their repeat business, making them less likely to switch to competitors.

Consistent Communication

Maintaining regular communication with clients helps to keep the business top-of-mind. Newsletters, email updates, and social media posts can provide clients with helpful information, exclusive offers, or behind-the-scenes insights. Communication should be meaningful, adding value to the client's experience rather than merely promoting sales. Regular interaction builds familiarity, fosters trust, and reminds clients of the brand, which can drive repeat purchases over time.

Quality Assurance

Delivering high-quality products or services consistently is crucial for retention. Clients need to trust that they will receive the same level of quality each time they engage with the business. Quality assurance measures, such as gathering client feedback and regularly reviewing product or service standards, demonstrate a commitment to excellence. When clients feel confident in the reliability of what they are buying, they are more likely to remain loyal.

> "Persistence is the twin sister of excellence. One is a matter of quality; the other, a matter of time." — Marabel Morgan

Seeking and Acting on Feedback

Asking for client feedback shows a commitment to improvement and makes clients feel heard. Small businesses can gather feedback through surveys, direct conversations, or online reviews. More importantly, they should act on this feedback, using it to make necessary adjustments or improvements. When clients see that their input directly affects business decisions, they feel a deeper connection to the brand and are more inclined to stay loyal.

In summary, both client retention and acquisition are vital to a business's success. However, prioritizing retention offers unique advantages, particularly for small businesses looking to build a stable revenue base and reduce marketing costs.

By focusing on exceptional customer service, personalization, loyalty programs, consistent communication, quality assurance, and feedback, small businesses can cultivate strong relationships with their clients, leading to sustained sales growth and profitability.

Chapter Recap

This chapter explored essential strategies for driving sales growth, covering concepts that support a business's profitability and market presence. Sales growth, defined as an increase in revenue over time, is crucial to sustaining a business, attracting investors, and fostering long-term success.

We began by clarifying the difference between clients and customers, noting that clients typically imply an ongoing, strategic relationship. Treating buyers as clients encourages a culture of loyalty, fostering long-term engagement.

Marketing strategy and planning were distinguished next, emphasizing that a marketing strategy sets the overall direction, while a marketing plan details the specific actions.

Branding emerged as another critical element, highlighting that a strong brand identity builds trust and sets a business apart from competitors.

Understanding one's target market and segmenting clients into specific groups allows for more focused and effective marketing efforts. Routes to market were discussed as strategic pathways, guiding how products reach clients, while pricing strategies were shown to impact client perception and buying behavior.

Finally, client retention was underscored as a key factor, often more cost-effective than client acquisition. Retention strategies like personalized service and loyalty programs increase lifetime client value and drive sustainable growth.

This chapter focused on the first of the three keys for profitability, namely sales.

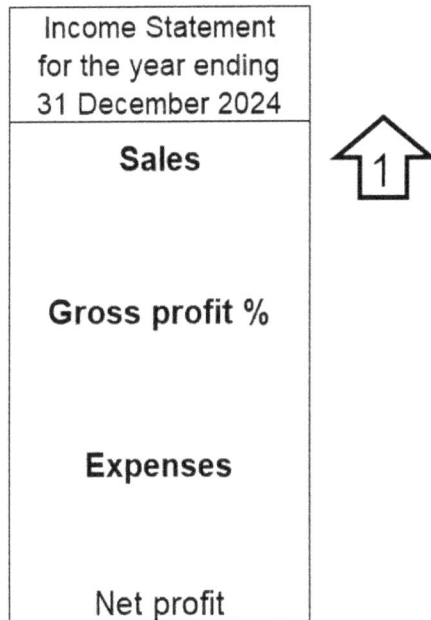

Image 2.1: Improving sales for profitability.

Action Plan

To unlock sales growth, you can follow these steps:

Identify Your Target Market: Define your ideal client by analyzing demographics, buying behaviors, and needs. This step helps you create tailored messages and strategies to engage the right audience effectively.

Segment Your Client Base: Divide your target market into smaller groups with shared characteristics. Use this segmentation to personalize your marketing efforts, making them more relevant and impactful.

Refine Your Brand Identity: Ensure that your branding aligns with your market positioning. Consistently communicate your brand values and voice across all platforms to build trust and recognition.

Choose the Best Routes to Market: Select strategic pathways to deliver your product or service to clients. Based on client preferences and your brand's goals, consider direct sales, partnerships, or online channels.

Set a Competitive Pricing Strategy: Choose a pricing model that reflects value without compromising profit. Avoid lowering prices unnecessarily; instead, emphasize quality and uniqueness to attract clients.

Focus on Client Retention: Implement retention strategies like loyalty programs, personalized service, and consistent communication to build lasting client relationships.

Chapter 3

Mastering Gross Profit

"Profit follows when you understand what clients value and consistently deliver it" – Jeffrey Pfeffer

Overview

Gross profit is a vital measure of business performance, yet it's often misunderstood. It reflects the profitability of core operations by showing the difference between revenue and the cost of goods sold (COGS). For small business owners, understanding gross profit is crucial—it's the first indicator of efficiency in production and sales. This chapter begins by defining gross profit and explaining its importance as a foundation for financial health. By analyzing gross profit, business owners can identify where adjustments might improve profitability.

One common point of confusion is the difference between markup and gross profit. While these terms are related, they serve different purposes and should not be used interchangeably. Markup refers to the percentage added to the cost of a product to determine its selling price, whereas gross profit is the remaining amount after COGS is subtracted from sales. Misunderstanding these concepts can lead to pricing errors that hurt profitability. We'll clarify these terms to help you apply each correctly.

An accurate calculation of gross profit relies on a thorough understanding of COGS. It includes the direct costs associated with producing or delivering a product or service. These costs vary by industry and can consist of materials, labor, and overhead. By breaking down COGS, business owners can gain insight into how production costs impact gross profit, allowing them to pinpoint opportunities for improvement.

Finally, we'll explore practical strategies to improve gross profit margins. Small adjustments, such as negotiating supplier contracts or optimizing production processes, can have a significant impact. By enhancing gross profit, businesses can strengthen their financial foundation without relying solely on increasing sales.

This chapter will equip you with the tools to assess and optimize gross profit, ultimately contributing to a healthier bottom line.

What is Gross Profit?

Gross profit is a fundamental financial metric used by businesses worldwide, and its core meaning remains consistent across countries.

Gross profit refers to the revenue a business generates minus its direct costs of production or sales. It represents the profit a company makes before deducting operating expenses, interest, and taxes. This metric provides a clear view of how efficiently a business generates profit from its core activities and indicates how well it manages its production costs in relation to its sales.

Gross profit will be used so often in this and the remaining chapters that we will often refer to it simply as *GP*.

Gross profit is not only a measure of current performance but also a tool for strategic decision-making. In industries with straightforward cost structures, gross profit is easy to calculate.

However, some sectors involve complex cost structures or unique revenue models, which can affect the way gross profit is reported. For instance, manufacturers might need to include the costs of raw materials, labor, and overhead, while a service-based business would consider direct labor and any materials used. Despite these differences, accounting standards such as GAAP[1] in the US and IFRS[2] internationally provide guidelines for calculating and reporting GP, ensuring consistency and comparability across industries and companies.

Gross profit is crucial for several reasons. For one, it allows business owners to see how effectively they're covering their direct costs. This insight can guide pricing strategies and help determine whether cost-saving measures are necessary. However, the importance of GP goes beyond internal decision-making. Lenders and investors pay close attention to GP when evaluating a business. If you ever need to raise funds, your gross profit margin will be scrutinized closely, whether you're seeking a loan or looking for investors. A substantial gross profit margin indicates that a business can generate profits from its operations, making it a lower-risk investment.

Similarly, if you decide to sell your business, potential buyers will carefully examine your gross profit margin. A higher GP suggests that the business has a competitive advantage, such as lower costs or efficient production processes. This competitive edge can enhance the value of the business in the eyes of buyers, who want to ensure that the business can sustain profitability. GP is a critical factor in business valuations, often making a significant difference

---

1. **GAAP:** Generally Accepted Accounting Principles. A set of accounting rules and standards used in the United States for financial reporting.

2. **IFRS:** International Financial Reporting Standards. A set of accounting standards used by most countries outside of the United States.

to the final sale price.

In summary, gross profit is not just a number on a financial statement. It's a powerful indicator of operational efficiency and financial health. Understanding and improving this metric can have a lasting impact on a business's success, both in daily operations and in long-term financial planning.

Calculating COGS

Before we proceed with the discussion on gross profit, we need to cover the Cost of Goods Sold (COGS). COGS represents the direct costs associated with procuring or producing goods sold by a company, including the cost of materials and direct labor. Calculating COGS varies in complexity, depending on the business type. A small retailer, for example, may find it relatively straightforward, while manufacturers often face a more intricate process involving multiple cost factors.

Inventory vs. Stock

In understanding COGS, it's essential to clarify the terms "inventory" and "stock." While often used interchangeably, these terms have subtle differences that can aid in more precise communication. Inventory, mainly used in accounting, refers to goods and materials held for sale or production. Stock, on the other hand, is a more casual term typically used in everyday business conversations. Although these distinctions exist, the two terms can usually be used interchangeably without significant differences in meaning. Recognizing these nuances helps maintain clarity in both internal and external communication.

Retail

For retail businesses, calculating COGS is straightforward. It involves determining the cost of inventory sold over a given period. The basic formula is:

COGS = Opening Stock + Purchases - Closing Stock

This method simply tracks inventory flow, from opening to closing balances, with any purchases added along the way. For retailers, it provides a clear view of how much stock has been sold and the associated costs, making it easier to assess profitability.

Manufacturing

Calculating COGS is more complex for manufacturers. Two primary costing methods are typically applied: Absorption Costing (or Full Costing) and Variable Costing.

Absorption Costing is a comprehensive approach to costing, incorporating all costs related to production. It includes three main elements:

1. Direct Materials: The raw materials used in production.

2. Direct Labor: The labor costs directly associated with manufacturing the product.

3. Manufacturing Overhead: Indirect costs related to production, such as utilities and rent related to manufacturing and equipment depreciation.

The formula for COGS under absorption costing is as follows:

COGS = Beginning Finished Goods Inventory + Cost of Goods Manufactured (COGM) - Ending Finished Goods Inventory

In turn, **COGM** is calculated as:

COGM = Beginning Work-in-Process Inventory + Direct Materials Used + Direct Labor + Manufacturing Overhead - Ending Work-in-Process Inventory

Efficiently implementing absorption costing requires robust policies, procedures, processes, and an equally robust accounting system. These elements ensure accuracy and consistency in cost tracking and reporting.

Absorption costing provides a complete picture of production costs by including all related expenses. This method aligns with GAAP and IFRS standards, making it suitable for financial reporting. Additionally, it offers a realistic view of profitability by incorporating all costs, allowing managers to make informed decisions about pricing and profitability.

Variable Costing is a more straightforward method that includes only variable costs, such as direct materials and direct labor while excluding manufacturing overhead from product costs. This approach allows for a focus on costs that fluctuate directly with production levels. It includes two main elements:

1. Direct Materials: The raw materials used in production.

2. Direct Labor: The labor costs directly associated with manufacturing the product.

Variable costing provides clear insights into the cost structure by isolating variable costs, which can aid in short-term decision-making. However, because it excludes fixed overhead, this method may offer a limited view of total production costs. While useful for internal purposes, variable costing is not compliant with GAAP or IFRS for external reporting.

Costing for Small Manufacturers

Small manufacturers often adopt a simplified approach to costing by focusing primarily on direct material costs and treating all other costs as operating expenses. Known as **simplified costing**, this method is practical for small businesses with straightforward production processes and limited overhead.

This approach works well for small manufacturers for several reasons:

Simplicity: Simplified costing reduces the need for complex calculations, making record-keeping more manageable.

Focus on Key Costs: By concentrating on direct materials, small businesses can easily track the primary cost driver of their products.

Quick Financial Insights: This method provides quick insights, aiding profitability and pricing decisions.

Despite its simplicity, this approach may not provide an accurate view of total production costs, especially if overhead is significant. It can also hinder precise decision-making, affecting pricing and product mix choices. Additionally, simplified costing may not meet external reporting standards such as GAAP or IFRS, which could become an issue as the business grows. As a small manufacturer scales up, adopting a more advanced method like absorption costing may be necessary to maintain accuracy and meet compliance standards.

Service Businesses

For service-based businesses, COGS is often replaced by the term **Cost of Revenue** or **Cost of Services Sold**. Since service businesses don't usually produce tangible goods, their cost structures differ. Costs directly associated with providing services generally include the following:

1. **Labor Costs**: This includes the wages and salaries of employees directly involved in delivering the service.

2. **Contract Labor Costs**: For outsourced or freelance services, fees paid to contractors are included in the cost.

3. **Direct Materials**: For some service businesses, specific materials are essential. For example, a hair salon may include hair products, or a consulting firm may account for supplies as direct materials.

By focusing on these costs, service businesses can track and manage their profitability effectively, even without traditional inventory or stock. Calculating the cost of revenue provides a framework similar to COGS for service-based businesses, allowing them to assess profitability on a service-by-service basis.

In summary, calculating COGS varies based on business type and complexity. Retailers typically have a straightforward calculation, while manufacturers might choose between absorption and variable costing, depending on their needs and compliance requirements. For small manufacturers, a simplified approach may suffice initially but may need to evolve as the business grows.

Service businesses, although different, can use the cost of revenue to achieve similar insights into their financial health. Understanding the nuances of COGS calculation helps business owners make more informed decisions and better manage profitability.

Calculating Gross Profit

With the Cost of Goods Sold (COGS) accurately calculated, we can move to the crux of this chapter—Gross Profit (GP). GP represents the profit a business makes from sales after covering the direct costs of production or procurement. This metric provides insight into operational efficiency, showing how effectively a business turns sales into profit before factoring in operating expenses. Calculating GP accurately is essential for understanding profitability and making informed financial decisions.

Retailers

For retail businesses, the GP calculation is straightforward. After determining the COGS, the formula to calculate GP is:

Sales – COGS = GP

This calculation clearly shows profitability derived directly from selling products. Retailers can use this GP figure to understand how well their product pricing covers the cost of goods sold, which is key to maintaining a sustainable profit margin.

Large Manufacturers

In manufacturing, GP calculation follows the same formula:

Sales – COGS = GP

However, manufacturing businesses may use either absorption costing or variable costing to determine COGS, which affects how GP is interpreted. If using absorption costing, the calculated GP reflects profit before subtracting non-manufacturing operating expenses, such as administrative salaries and office expenses.

With variable costing, however, GP accounts only for variable costs (direct material and labor), meaning that related manufacturing costs—like rent and utilities for the production facility—are included in the operating expenses.

Small Manufacturers

For small manufacturers, the formula remains:

Sales – COGS = GP

However, this GP typically only covers the cost of materials. Other costs, such as direct labor and manufacturing overhead, are generally grouped with operating expenses in simplified costing approaches.

This approach provides a clear, manageable way for small manufacturers to track profitability without the added complexity of allocating overhead costs to each product.

Service Businesses

For service businesses, calculating GP uses a similar formula, though the term Cost of Services Sold (COSS) replaces COGS. The formula is as follows:

Sales – COSS = GP

In service-based industries, COSS includes the direct costs of providing services, such as labor, contract fees, and materials specific to the service.

Calculating GP in this way allows service businesses to assess profitability by focusing on the direct costs related to service delivery.

Gross Profit per Unit

Thus far, GP calculations have reflected total profit for a given period—monthly or annually, whatever the case may be. In some cases, however, calculating GP on a per-unit basis is beneficial, as it provides insight into profitability for individual items or services. Knowing GP per unit helps in setting prices, assessing individual product performance, and making informed inventory or service adjustments.

For retailers, GP per unit is calculated by subtracting the per-unit cost from the sales price. In manufacturing, GP per unit requires dividing the total GP by the number of units produced and sold, which accounts for both material and production costs. For service businesses, GP per unit can be calculated by dividing the total GP by the number of service engagements or hours worked, offering insights into profitability for each client or project.

Gross Profit %

While the monetary value of GP is essential, it only tells part of the story. The Gross Profit Percentage (GP%) provides a more dynamic view by representing GP as a proportion of sales.

GP% is calculated as follows:

GP% = (GP ÷ Sales) × 100

This result literally indicates what portion of every sales dollar is GP, which goes into a pool of money to pay operating expenses, interest, and taxes.

GP% is crucial for tracking trends and benchmarking against industry standards or competitors. An increasing GP% suggests improved efficiency or profitability, while a declining GP% may indicate rising costs or pricing issues. Monitoring GP% over time helps businesses set realistic profit goals and identify potential problem areas.

Setting performance goals based on GP% rather than monetary GP is often more effective. This approach accounts for fluctuations in sales volumes, providing a consistent measure of profitability regardless of sales growth or decline.

Average GP%

The GP and GP% calculated for any period represent an average GP% across all products or services sold. For businesses with only one product or those offering items with identical GP%, the average GP% equals the product's GP%.

However, most businesses offer a mix of products with varying GP percentages.

To calculate an average GP%, business owners need to know how much each product, service, or department contributes to total sales. This weighted approach provides a more accurate view of overall profitability.

Example of Average GP% Calculation

Consider a small supermarket with four sections: Groceries, Cleaning Materials, Bakery, and Fresh Produce. Each section has a different GP% and contributes a specific percentage to total sales. Here's the data:

Groceries: GP% = 10%, Contribution to Sales = 40%

Cleaning Materials: GP% = 20%, Contribution to Sales = 30%

Bakery: GP% = 50%, Contribution to Sales = 10%

Fresh Produce: GP% = 30%, Contribution to Sales = 20%

Using this information, we can calculate the average GP% by multiplying each section's GP% by its sales contribution.

Section	GP%	Contribution to Sales	Contribution to GP%
Groceries	10%	40%	4%
Cleaning materials	20%	30%	6%
Bakery	50%	10%	5%
Fresh produce	30%	20%	6%
Total		100%	21%

The average GP% for the supermarket is 21%, calculated by summing the contribution to GP% for each section.

The Contribution to Sales represents the sales mix, which can impact GP. Although we'll explore sales mix strategies later, understanding how each segment contributes to total GP is essential.

Summary of Gross Profit Calculations

Calculating GP accurately depends on understanding COGS and aligning it with the business type. Retailers use a straightforward approach, while manufacturers may choose absorption or variable costing to suit their needs. Small manufacturers may simplify by focusing on direct material costs, and service businesses use Cost of Services Sold to calculate GP. Additionally, GP per unit offers insights into profitability at a product level, while GP% and average GP% provide broader performance perspectives, helping businesses set informed goals and track financial health over time.

Gross Profit vs. Markup

Before we discuss strategies for improving the Gross Profit Percentage (GP%), it's essential to understand the relationship between Gross Profit (GP) and Markup (MU).

While most prospective entrepreneurs and small business owners instinctively know what MU is, the technical differences between GP and MU—and their respective calculations—can be a source of confusion. We'll break down these differences using simple language and terms:

Cost Price (CP) – The amount paid to buy or produce a product.

Selling Price (SP) – The price at which the product is sold to clients.

Gross Profit (GP) – The profit left after subtracting CP from SP.

Gross Profit % (GP%) – GP expressed as a percentage of SP.

Markup (MU) – The amount added to CP to set the SP.

Markup % (MU%) – MU expressed as a percentage of CP.

These six terms illustrate the entire distinction between GP and MU, proving it's not overly complicated but essential to understand clearly.

To clarify, let's use a straightforward example. Imagine I buy a tablet used for casual reading at $100 and apply a markup of 50%. The calculation of SP would look like this:

Term	Value	Explanation
CP	$100	Cost Price of the tablet
MU%	50%	Markup Percentage
MU	$50	Markup Amount
SP	$150	Selling Price (CP + MU)

Once the SP is calculated, we can determine the GP and GP% as follows:

Term	Value	Explanation
SP	$150	Selling Price
CP	$100	Cost Price
GP	$50	Gross Profit (SP – CP)
GP%	33%	Gross Profit % (GP as a percentage of SP)

An interesting point to note is that MU and GP are the same in terms of money, both being $50. However, their percentages differ: MU is 50%, while GP is only 33%.

This is where people often get tripped up—the dollar amount may match, but the percentages diverge because they're calculated against different bases. MU is expressed as a percentage of CP, while GP is expressed as percentage of SP. Thus, although the money is identical, the percentages reflect different aspects of pricing and are calculated from different bases.

Term	Value		Explanation
CP	$100		Cost Price of the tablet
MU%	50%		Markup %
MU	$50		Markup Amount
SP	$150		Selling Price (CP + MU)

Same	Term	Value	Different	Explanation
	SP	$150		Selling Price
	CP	$100		Cost Price
	GP	$50		Gross Profit (SP – CP)
	GP%	33%		Gross Profit %

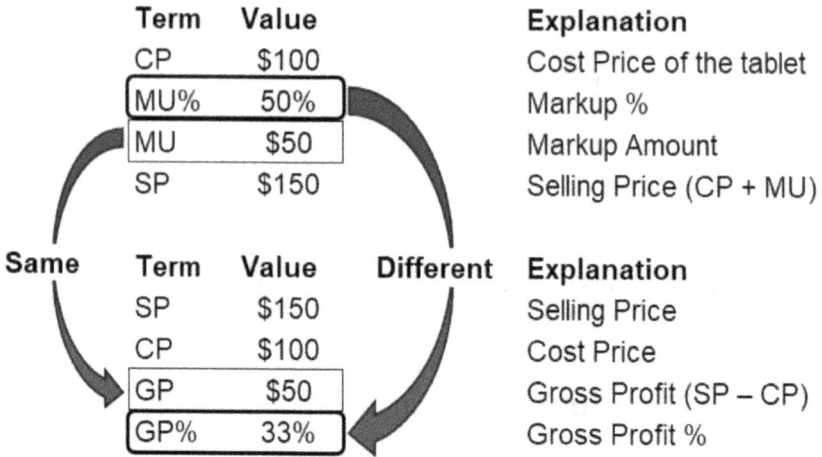

Image 3.1: Markup % vs. gross profit % illustrated.

To provide a quick reference, here's how GP% correlates to different MU%:

MU%	GP%
200%	66%
100%	50%
50%	33%
33%	25%
25%	20%
20%	17%

Understanding these differences is crucial for clear communication, whether within the business or when dealing with lenders and investors. As a financier, I've encountered many entrepreneurs saying, "I make 100% profit," which often leads to misunderstandings. This statement is both imprecise and misleading. Firstly, it's better to specify "gross profit percentage" or simply "gross margin." Secondly, a business can only achieve a GP% of 100% if COGS or Cost of Services Sold (COSS) is zero—something uncommon outside of certain small service businesses that categorize all costs as operating expenses. In any industry with COGS or COSS, the GP% will always be less than 100%, as shown in the table above.

In business discussions, it's fine to mention MU% instead of GP% as long as everyone understands the distinction. For example, you might say, "We apply a MU% of 200%," which is equivalent to stating, "We achieve a GP% of 66%." This level of clarity helps avoid confusion and sets realistic expectations around profitability.

To summarize, GP and MU, though related, have essential differences. Gross Profit measures the margin achieved after covering COGS, while Markup represents the added percentage over CP to set the SP. Both are valuable metrics but serve different purposes in evaluating and communicating profitability.

(i) In Appendix B: Resources, you will find a link to an Excel workbook containing many useful formulae and exercises around markup and gross profit. In that document, you can explore the conversion from MU% to GP% and vice versa and calculate the average GP%.

Improving the Gross Profit %

We've previously discussed the foundational concepts of Cost of Goods Sold (COGS) and Gross Profit (GP), both of which are essential to understanding profitability.

As a reminder, sales—whether over a period or for a specific product—comprise two main components: COGS and GP. GP represents the profit margin after covering the direct costs of goods sold, but it's not a static figure. Improving GP%, or Gross Profit Percentage, requires a strategic focus on changing two elements: sales and COGS. Since we explored ways to improve sales in the earlier chapter, this section will center on enhancing COGS.

Even modest adjustments in COGS can significantly boost GP%, creating more value for the business without necessarily increasing sales.

Improving COGS is not about finding one big solution but instead involves a series of small, consistent changes across the entire production or procurement process. Each business, due to its unique structure, industry, and costing models, has different elements that contribute to COGS. Therefore, a customized approach is essential for successful COGS reduction.

Here, we'll explore 18 strategies applicable to a wide range of businesses. These measures can be applied individually or collectively, helping business owners create a more streamlined and efficient cost structure. By systematically addressing these elements, a business can make long-term improvements in GP%.

Product Mix

The product mix is one of the most effective ways to decrease COGS and increase GP%. By focusing on products with higher margins, businesses can reduce the weighted average COGS across the product range. For instance, if a retail business shifts its focus from lower-margin staples to higher-margin specialty items, it can improve overall GP%. Take the example of a grocery store:

by adding gourmet products like organic jams or artisan cheeses, which often have higher markups, the store can increase GP% without significant operational changes.

Product Differentiation

Differentiating products gives a business pricing power, allowing it to set higher prices without facing heavy price competition. Unique or innovative products often justify a higher price, which translates to higher GP%. For example, a furniture manufacturer that sources eco-friendly materials and advertises sustainable practices can set itself apart from competitors by charging premium prices. By positioning products uniquely in the market, a business can build brand loyalty while improving profitability. In this way, product differentiation aligns with sustainability and meets consumer demand for responsible practices.

Negotiate with Suppliers

Revisiting supplier relationships is a fundamental strategy for reducing COGS. Every supplier, whether large or small, can potentially offer more favorable terms. Building solid relationships with suppliers may yield benefits such as lower per-unit costs, bulk discounts, or more flexible payment terms. For example, a bakery might negotiate with its flour supplier for discounts on bulk orders, reducing costs per unit.

Suppliers may also offer marketing support, such as promotional materials, samples, or co-branding opportunities. While these aspects belong more to the sales side, their indirect effect on reducing costs can contribute to higher GP%.

Shipping and Logistics Costs

Efficient logistics are essential to cost management, especially for product-based businesses with significant delivery expenses. Refining shipping routes and selecting the proper logistics providers can reduce transportation costs, thereby lowering COGS. For example, a regional distributor could centralize warehouses to shorten delivery distances, thereby reducing fuel expenses and improving delivery speed. Businesses might also negotiate better rates with logistics providers based on volume, achieving cost savings that directly affect GP%.

Operational Efficiency

Improving operational efficiency goes beyond streamlining processes; it also includes investing in automation and enhancing workflow, which can reduce labor costs and minimize waste. For example, a manufacturer may implement automation to speed up repetitive tasks, reducing human labor costs and error rates. Alternatively, a restaurant could improve the kitchen layout to enhance workflow, reducing time spent on each order and labor hours. These efficiency gains often lead to significant reductions in COGS, benefiting the GP% without requiring a sales increase.

Waste

Waste reduction is relevant to all business types, not just manufacturers. Waste adds costs without contributing value, making it a prime target for GP% improvement. For manufacturers, implementing lean manufacturing principles can reduce material waste. For instance, a printing company that repurposes excess paper stock for smaller jobs or secondary uses can save significantly on raw materials. Service-oriented businesses can also reduce waste; for example, a consulting firm can digitize client reports and communications to cut down on printing and storage costs, enhancing profitability.

Product Quality

Improving product quality directly reduces COGS by decreasing returns, complaints, and warranty claims, which all come with added costs. High-quality products also support premium pricing, allowing for better profit margins. For example, an electronics manufacturer that implements strict quality controls can reduce faulty returns, save on repair costs, and maintain client loyalty. Consistent quality often supports a brand's reputation and justifies premium prices, creating a buffer for GP%.

Labor Costs

Optimizing labor productivity is essential for reducing COGS. By regularly evaluating productivity and adjusting to reduce overtime or improve scheduling, businesses can reduce costs without affecting output. For example, a retail store might create optimized shift schedules based on peak hours, ensuring labor costs align with demand.

Cross-training employees is also effective, allowing team members to cover multiple roles, which can reduce the need for extra staff.

Inventory Management

Inventory optimization is critical to minimize holding costs and prevent obsolescence. Strategies like just-in-time (JIT) inventory and demand forecasting can help businesses reduce excess stock and improve cash flow. A clothing retailer that uses JIT inventory to manage seasonal trends can avoid markdowns and maintain higher profit margins.

Effective inventory management systems prevent overstock and ensure products meet demand without the risk of tying up capital unnecessarily.

Other Causes of Obsolescence

Obsolescence isn't limited to physical wear and tear; it can also stem from changing consumer preferences, technological advancements, or regulatory updates. For instance, a mobile phone manufacturer must adapt quickly to innovative technology or risk outdated stock. A food manufacturer may face obsolescence due to changing health regulations, which might require ingredient changes. By staying attuned to these risks, businesses can reduce losses from obsolete inventory, positively impacting COGS and GP%.

Pilferage and Shoplifting

Pilferage and shoplifting are indirect costs that affect COGS and, ultimately, GP%. Though often associated with retail, pilferage can occur in any industry, including services. The National Retail Federation[3] reports that pilferage in large supermarkets accounts for 1-2% of total sales. Strategies to reduce these losses include security systems, employee training, and inventory audits. By implementing strong anti-theft measures, businesses can safeguard assets and improve GP%.

---

3. The National Retail Federation (NRF) is a US organization. It's the world's largest retail trade association, representing retailers of all types from the United States and over 45 countries. However, its headquarters are in Washington, D.C., USA.

Value-Added Services

Value-added services allow businesses to justify higher prices without significantly increasing costs. For example, a retail store could offer premium packaging or delivery options, enhancing the client experience and creating an opportunity for upselling. In manufacturing, a company might provide customization or extended warranties, allowing for a slight price increase that doesn't add significant costs.

These services enhance perceived value and can directly affect GP%.

Outsourcing

Outsourcing non-core functions can reduce labor costs and overhead, allowing businesses to concentrate on high-margin products. For instance, a small IT firm might outsource client support, reducing payroll expenses and freeing up resources for specialized work.

Outsourcing non-core tasks often allows businesses to focus on profitable areas, improving GP% while maintaining quality.

Sales Mix

Sales mix adjustments influence GP% by prioritizing high-margin items over lower-margin ones. For instance, a supermarket could adjust its sales mix by focusing more on high-margin organic or imported products, thus increasing the average GP%.

Understanding client preferences and stocking accordingly helps improve GP% through subtle shifts in inventory strategy.

Effective Sales Training

Sales training that emphasizes high-margin products and upselling can improve GP% without impacting COGS. For example, a car dealership might train sales staff to highlight premium add-ons or upgrades, boosting revenue without added cost. Effective sales techniques help align the sales mix with higher-margin items, enhancing overall profitability.

Pricing Strategy

Pricing directly impacts both sales and GP%. While price increases must be carefully managed to avoid reducing demand, they can be highly effective for high-demand, high-margin items. For instance, a coffee shop might introduce a new premium roast at a higher price, appealing to connoisseurs willing to pay more. Strategic pricing adjustments contribute to an improved GP% while maintaining client satisfaction.

Discounts

Discounts can have a significant negative impact on GP%, and their effect cannot be overstated. When SP is reduced (due to a discount) but COGS stays the same, GP decreases. Therefore, businesses must set discount limits through a Maximum Discount % calculation, ensuring profitability even during promotions.

There are two levels of maximum discount. Firstly, a business might decide to give a discount so large that the discounted sales price would only cover COGS, leaving a gross profit of zero. In this case, the maximum discount % would be the same as the GP% on that specific product. In this case the operating costs (indirect overheads) are not covered and that discount % will result in a net loss.

Secondly, and more prudently, the business wants to give the maximum discount possible but still cover COGS as well as the operating costs (those indirect overheads) associated with a product. This calculation depends on the total sales amount, gross profit percentage, and operating costs.

The formula is $1-((Sales \times (1-GP\%) + Operating\ Costs)/Sales)$. This result will always be a % smaller than the GP% to allow the business to cover operating costs.

When it comes to discounts, please remember the age-old wisdom: Sales are vanity, profit is sanity.

(i) The Excel workbook in Appendix B: Resources includes exercises on discounts and helps calculate safe discount levels.

Use Technology for Data-Driven Decisions

Using technology and data analytics offers real-time insights into sales, inventory, and pricing, allowing immediate actions that can improve GP%. For example, a retail store using data analytics can identify high-margin items that sell well and adjust inventory accordingly. Real-time insights allow businesses to make informed decisions and adjust quickly to maximize GP%.

In conclusion, improving GP% involves optimizing various elements of COGS through targeted strategies. The 18 approaches discussed here offer a holistic way to manage costs, from negotiating supplier terms to enhancing product quality and training sales teams. These cumulative efforts can create lasting improvements in GP%, positioning the business for sustained profitability.

A Word on Quality

While we discuss product quality as a method to reduce the Cost of Goods Sold (COGS), this conversation goes beyond accounting. Quality is a business philosophy and a long-term strategy. It's about understanding that while cost-cutting measures may yield short-term savings, sustainable profitability is often built on a foundation of quality. In the long run, quality always trumps price. Low prices may attract clients, but they stay loyal to brands that deliver reliability, durability, and consistency.

> **"** "A business that makes nothing but money is a poor business" – Henry Ford **"**

Steve Jobs, co-founder of Apple, once famously said, "Quality is more important than quantity. One home run is much better than two doubles" (Source: *"Steve Jobs" by Walter Isaacson*). Jobs's philosophy drove Apple to create high-quality products that became industry leaders, commanding premium prices and fostering brand loyalty. By prioritizing quality, businesses can differentiate themselves from competitors, ultimately allowing them to sustain higher gross profit percentages.

Quality also creates a ripple effect: it reduces returns, minimizes warranty claims, and lowers support costs, all of which contribute to a leaner COGS in the long term.

Investing in quality may have higher upfront costs, but it creates value that pays off as products with a formidable reputation build trust with clients. This trust, in turn, provides pricing power that enables a business to achieve robust profit margins while cultivating a loyal client base.

Chapter Recap

In this chapter, we explored the concept of Gross Profit (GP) and its relationship with Cost of Goods Sold (COGS). We examined how GP serves as a critical metric, reflecting the profitability derived from core trading activities before accounting for operating expenses. Understanding and accurately calculating COGS is foundational to determining GP. By calculating COGS correctly, businesses can uncover meaningful insights into their cost structure, providing the first step towards improving GP%.

We also discussed various strategies to enhance the Gross Profit Percentage (GP%). Given that GP is a function of both sales and COGS, improving GP% requires a balanced approach that targets both elements. In this chapter, we focused on improving COGS by addressing specific cost-related factors. Some of these strategies included refining the product mix, improving supplier relationships, reducing waste, enhancing inventory management, and investing in product quality. Each of these elements contributes incrementally to reducing COGS and, in turn, raising GP%.

In addition, we covered the impact of product differentiation, labor productivity, and the role of practical sales training in enhancing GP%. Strategies like keeping an efficient sales mix, employing value-added services, and carefully considering discount policies also contribute significantly to profitability.

By combining these strategies, businesses can create a stronger foundation for long-term profitability, leveraging the power of a higher GP% to maintain competitive advantages. This chapter serves as a practical guide for business owners aiming to achieve sustainable profitability through focused, incremental improvements in cost management and operational efficiency.

This chapter focused on the second of the three keys, namely gross profit percentage.

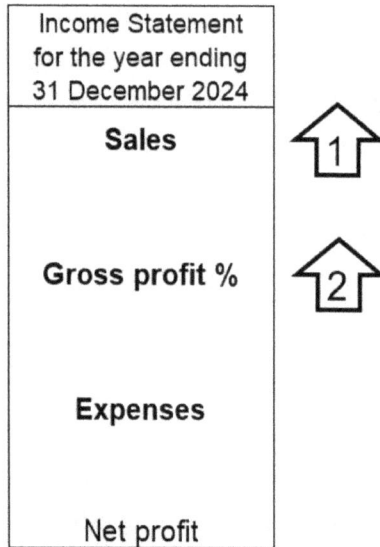

Image 3.2: Improving the GP% for profitability.

Action Plan

Small business owners should assess their current Cost of Goods Sold (COGS) structure to improve their gross profit percentage (GP%).

Begin with a detailed breakdown of COGS, identifying all cost elements and their impact on profitability.

Set a GP% target that aligns with your business goals and industry standards. Once you have clarity on your baseline and goals, prioritize areas for improvement.

Focus on incremental, sustainable changes rather than one-time cost-cutting. Implement as many of the 18 approaches discussed in the chapter.

Make it a point to regularly review pricing and discount strategies and align them with your desired GP%, adapting them as your business and market conditions change.

Finally, track your progress with regular GP% evaluations. Minor adjustments over time will compound, creating a stronger, more profitable foundation for your business.

Chapter 4
Managing Expenses Efficiently

"Without profit, no business can grow, no company can innovate, and no economy can thrive" – Peter Drucker

Overview

Managing expenses efficiently is the third key of profitability we're exploring in this book. After examining sales and gross profit, it's time to focus on cost control—a crucial element for boosting the bottom line. Every dollar saved on expenses directly improves profitability, making it essential to understand and optimize where your money goes. Effective expense management requires an organized, systematic approach that aligns with your business goals.

In this chapter, we'll begin with a breakdown of fixed versus variable expenses. Fixed expenses are consistent and predictable, like rent or salaries, while variable expenses change with production or sales levels. Recognizing the difference helps you assess which costs can be adjusted in the short term versus those that require long-term planning.

Next, we'll cover the break-even point, a vital concept for any business owner. Knowing your break-even point allows you to see exactly how much revenue you need to cover all expenses. By reducing costs, you can reach profitability sooner, which is essential during challenging economic periods.

The chapter also dives into expense control strategies. From outsourcing to automating, there are several ways to reduce unnecessary costs without sacrificing quality. We'll discuss the nuances of managing fixed and variable expenses, helping you implement targeted approaches for each.

Lastly, we'll cover the balance between cutting costs and investing for growth. Some expenses, like capital expenditures (CapEx) and operational expenses (OpEx), are crucial for future success. Understanding where to invest and where to save ensures a healthy balance for sustainable growth.

What Expenses Are We Talking About?

In this chapter, we're focusing on a critical component of profitability: expenses. For clarity, we'll use "expenses" to mean operating costs or operating expenses, excluding those directly tied to producing or procuring goods sold.

Previously, in our discussion on gross profit, we covered the *Cost of Goods Sold (COGS)* and *Cost of Services Sold (COSS)*, which account for production-related costs. Since businesses vary widely—from manufacturing to services—and use different costing methods like absorption or simplified costing, it's essential to define what expenses we're covering here.

Expenses, as discussed in this chapter, include all costs outside COGS or COSS. These expenses must be covered by gross profit before reaching net profit. Understanding and managing these costs effectively can have a substantial impact on overall profitability.

For example, in a **manufacturer using absorption costing**, expenses outside COGS might include administrative salaries, office rent, and sales and marketing expenses. Absorption costing incorporates manufacturing overhead (like factory rent) into COGS, so the expenses we discuss here are primarily non-manufacturing.

For a **manufacturer using variable costing**, expenses typically include fixed overhead costs. Unlike absorption costing, variable costing only incorporates variable production costs within COGS. As a result, fixed overhead, administrative costs, and other selling expenses must be covered by gross profit.

In a **manufacturer using simplified costing**, the expenses may be more straightforward to manage, but they still include operational costs outside direct material and labor. Simplified costing often treats overhead as an operating expense, meaning items like facility maintenance, general administration, and marketing costs fall under this chapter's scope.

In a **retail business**, expenses usually involve operational costs that are not linked to inventory purchases. Examples include store rent, utility bills, employee wages, and advertising costs. These expenses are critical to running the business, yet they don't directly contribute to the sale of goods. Managing these costs well is essential for improving profitability.

Finally, in a **service business**, expenses cover any costs not included in COSS. Service-based companies have fewer production costs, so their COSS may include wages for direct labor or materials used. The remaining expenses, such as office supplies, insurance, and general administration, must be paid from gross profit.

Each business type faces a unique mix of expenses, yet all share the goal of managing these costs to maximize net profit. By understanding what expenses we're addressing, you'll be better equipped to optimize them, ensuring a more efficient, profitable operation.

Fixed vs. Variable Expenses

In managing expenses, it's vital to differentiate between *fixed* and *variable* expenses—those costs that fall outside the Cost of Goods Sold (COGS) and must be covered by gross profit. **Fixed expenses** are costs that stay constant over time, unaffected by changes in sales or production levels. Examples include rent, loan payments, and certain administrative salaries. These expenses are predictable and remain the same regardless of how much a business sells or produces. On the other hand, **variable expenses** fluctuate in direct relation to business activity. As sales or production increases, variable expenses also rise, and they decrease when business activity slows. Common examples of variable expenses include sales commissions, shipping and handling costs, and marketing expenses.

The distinction between fixed and variable expenses impacts profitability because each affects cash flow differently. **Fixed expenses** provide stability, as they are consistent, making it easier to budget for long-term planning. As revenue increases, the impact of each fixed cost per unit sold decreases, effectively lowering the cost burden per unit and boosting net profit. However, when revenue declines, fixed expenses remain the same, which can strain cash flow. In contrast, **variable expenses** scale with business activity, so during periods of lower revenue, these costs also drop. This alignment offers flexibility, allowing businesses to adjust spending according to revenue fluctuations.

An expense's classification as fixed or variable often depends on its relationship to the business's sales and operations. Fixed expenses generally cover essential costs necessary to keep the business running but are not directly tied to the volume of sales or production. For instance, an office lease is a fixed expense since it doesn't change regardless of sales. Variable expenses, however, fluctuate with revenue, often covering costs that increase as more products are sold or more services are provided.

Determining whether fixed or variable expenses are preferable depends on the business model and financial goals. **Fixed expenses** are beneficial for budgeting and offer predictability, which is helpful for long-term planning. However, high fixed costs can become a burden during slow periods, as they still need to be covered even if sales decline. **Variable expenses**, by contrast, provide flexibility. Since they change with business activity, they allow costs to adjust in line with revenue, which can be advantageous during unpredictable periods. A balanced approach that incorporates both types strategically can help maintain profitability across varying market conditions.

Consider a detailed example of a **fixed expense**: office rent. Regardless of how many products are sold, the rent payment remains constant each month. This consistency is beneficial for planning but requires reliable revenue to ensure that the business can always cover the cost. In times of low revenue, fixed expenses like rent can place pressure on cash flow.

Now, let's look at **variable expenses** with two examples. First, sales commissions, which are typically paid as a percentage of sales. When sales are high, commission expenses increase, and they drop when sales decline, making them an actual variable cost. Second, marketing and advertising expenses are often flexible. During a product launch or peak sales period, marketing spending may rise to drive awareness and sales. In slower periods, however, marketing costs can be reduced, adapting to the business's revenue flow. Another example of a variable expense might be waste removal fees, especially if charged by volume. As production levels vary, so does the waste generated, which directly impacts these costs.

It's also possible to change certain fixed expenses into variable ones. For instance, a company might outsource administrative services, like IT support, instead of maintaining in-house staff. In doing so, they pay only for the services they use, converting a fixed payroll expense into a variable service cost. This shift provides flexibility by allowing the business to align its expenses with current operational needs.

By understanding fixed and variable expenses, businesses can make strategic decisions that align costs with revenue, improving resilience and long-term profitability.

Breakeven Analysis

Breakeven analysis is a fundamental tool for any business owner. It allows them to understand the level of sales needed to cover all expenses and reach a point where they begin generating profit. In simple terms, breakeven is the sales amount required for a business to avoid losses—where total revenue matches total expenses.

For investors and financial analysts, breakeven is a precise measure indicating the point at which the business's operating income covers both its fixed and variable costs. This concept is crucial for assessing a company's financial stability and long-term profitability potential.

In the second book of this series, *Business Entry: Starting vs Buying*, reaching breakeven is highlighted as the single most crucial milestone after setting up operations and launching the business.

Without achieving breakeven, a business cannot sustain itself long-term, as continuous losses erode cash reserves and threaten solvency. Thus, breakeven serves as a critical marker for survival, especially in the early stages of a business. Achieving breakeven gives business owners confidence, reassures investors, and sets the foundation for future profitability.

Breakeven analysis is essential for several reasons. Firstly, it provides a clear financial goal by quantifying how much a business needs to sell to cover its costs. This clarity is precious when setting sales targets or designing marketing strategies. Secondly, breakeven analysis helps assess risk. By understanding the sales level required to cover expenses, business owners can evaluate whether their revenue projections are realistic and, if necessary, adjust their cost structure. Additionally, breakeven analysis assists in pricing decisions, as it reveals the impact of different price points on the required sales volume. This insight ensures that pricing strategies align with cost structures, leading to more sustainable profit margins.

Two Levels of Breakeven Calculation

Breakeven calculations vary depending on the business model. There are two primary levels or approaches to calculating breakeven: one for businesses with all fixed expenses and another for those with a mix of fixed and variable expenses.

Breakeven for Businesses with All Fixed Expenses

For businesses with primarily fixed expenses and little or no variable costs, the breakeven formula is straightforward:

Breakeven Sales = Total Expenses / Gross Profit %

In this case, fixed expenses remain constant regardless of sales volume. Let's look at a practical example. Suppose a consulting firm has fixed expenses of $60,000 per month and a gross profit percentage of 50%. The calculation would be as follows:

Breakeven Sales = 60,0000 / 50% = 120,000

This calculation shows that the consulting firm needs $120,000 in monthly sales to fully cover its expenses and reach breakeven. Because this business has only fixed expenses, the breakeven analysis is simple. However, most businesses also incur variable expenses, which makes the calculation a bit more complex.

Breakeven for Businesses with Mixed Expenses (Fixed and Variable)

For businesses with both fixed and variable expenses, breakeven calculation takes on an added layer. Here, variable expenses—such as commissions, shipping, or marketing—fluctuate with sales volume. In this case, the formula is modified to account for the impact of variable costs on breakeven:

Breakeven Sales = Fixed Expenses / (Gross Profit % - Variable Expense %), where the Variable Expense % is the variable expenses as a percentage of sales.

Let's apply this formula with an example. Assume a retail business has $40,000 in fixed expenses, a gross profit percentage of 60%, and a variable expense percentage of 15%. The calculation would be:

Breakeven Sales = 40,0000 / (60% - 15%) = 88,889

In this example, the business needs $88,889 in sales to break even. Because the variable expenses adjust with each sale, they reduce the effective gross profit margin, requiring the business to achieve a higher sales target to cover both fixed and variable costs.

Key Elements Influencing Breakeven: Expenses and Gross Profit Percentage

Two main factors determine breakeven sales: expenses and gross profit percentage (GP%). In the previous chapter, we explored GP% and its impact on profitability. A higher GP% means that more of each sales dollar contributes to covering expenses, thus lowering the breakeven point. Now, our focus is on expenses, which play an equally crucial role in reaching breakeven.

Managing expenses effectively can lower the breakeven point, making it easier for a business to achieve profitability. When fixed expenses are high, the business must generate a larger sales volume to cover those costs. Conversely, reducing fixed expenses can decrease the sales required to break even. Variable expenses also impact breakeven, as they consume a portion of each sales dollar. Controlling these expenses—by negotiating better rates for shipping or refining marketing strategies—can decrease expenses and lower breakeven sales.

Example: Impact of Reducing Expenses on Breakeven Sales

To illustrate, let's examine how reducing expenses affects breakeven. Suppose a business initially has fixed expenses of $70,000, a GP% of 50%, and a variable expense percentage of 10%. The breakeven calculation would be as follows:

Breakeven Sales = 70,0000 / (50% - 10%) = 175,000

In this scenario, the business needs $175,000 in sales to break even. Now, let's assume the business finds ways to reduce fixed expenses by $5,000, bringing them down to $65,000. Recalculating the breakeven point with the reduced expenses:

Breakeven Sales = 65,0000 / (50% - 10%) = 162,500

With the reduced fixed expenses, the breakeven sales target drops to $162,500, a $12,500 decrease. This example illustrates how managing expenses, especially fixed costs, directly influences breakeven and helps the business reach profitability faster.

Breakeven as a % of Sales

Breakeven as a percentage of sales is a valuable metric for evaluating a business's financial health, stability, and risk. For small businesses, the lower this percentage, the healthier and more stable the business tends to be. A lower breakeven percentage indicates a wider margin between current sales and the amount needed to cover costs, providing a cushion for profitability and growth. Here's a guideline for interpreting breakeven as a percentage of sales in terms of risk:

Start-ups: Typically, above 100%

New businesses often experience high initial costs and low sales volume. In this phase, the breakeven percentage will usually be well above 100% of sales. As the business grows and sales increase, the percentage should gradually approach 100%, indicating a stable base. Any further increase in sales will drop the percentage below 100%, moving the business closer to profitability.

High Risk / Dangerous: Above 85%

A breakeven point above 85% of sales places a business in a high-risk category. This level indicates a narrow profit margin, where most of the current sales are required just to cover costs, leaving minimal room for profit. Any downturn in sales or unexpected expenses could quickly lead to losses. For businesses in this range, it is critical to reduce expenses or increase gross profit margins to lower the breakeven point.

Medium Risk / Acceptable: 70% - 85%

Breakeven in this range reflects moderate risk. The business is covering its expenses but without significant flexibility. There is some margin for profit, but any dip in sales could impact profitability. Although manageable, this level suggests that additional measures—such as optimizing expenses or improving profit margins—could enhance financial stability.

Low Risk / Good: Below 70%

Breakeven below 70% of sales indicates strong financial health. At this level, the business covers its costs well below its total sales, creating a substantial buffer for profitability and growth. This lower breakeven percentage reflects stability, resilience to market changes, and the potential for reinvestment or expansion.

For small businesses, maintaining a breakeven percentage below 70% of sales is ideal. This target ensures the flexibility needed to manage market fluctuations, reinvest in the business, and build long-term stability.

A breakeven percentage above 85%, however, signals a need for closer cost control and profitability adjustments.

(i) The Excel workbook in Appendix B: Resources includes exercises on breakeven sales.

Importance of Breakeven for Business Success

Reaching breakeven is a crucial milestone in any business, as it represents the point where the business becomes financially self-sustaining. This analysis informs pricing strategies, cost management, and sales goals, as each element affects the sales volume required to break even.

Breakeven analysis also has strategic importance. For new businesses, reaching breakeven as soon as possible reduces the strain on capital and attracts investor confidence. In established businesses, breakeven analysis helps monitor ongoing financial health, guiding operational decisions that prevent cash flow issues.

Whether starting up or scaling, understanding the path to breakeven provides clear financial direction, helping businesses plan for both growth and stability.

By focusing on both keys discussed in the last two chapters—GP% and expenses—businesses can actively manage their breakeven point, ensuring they stay on track to achieve long-term profitability. A clear grasp of breakeven offers more than just a financial checkpoint; it provides a foundational strategy for sustaining and growing a successful business.

Expense Control

Expense control is a critical aspect of managing profitability, especially when we focus on expenses that fall outside the Cost of Goods Sold (COGS). These are costs that must be covered by the gross profit (GP) to ensure the business reaches net profitability.

By controlling these expenses, we can decrease the breakeven point, lower the risk of financial strain, and improve net profit (NP). Now that we have a solid understanding of breakeven analysis and a practical Excel model to evaluate various scenarios, we can genuinely appreciate how reducing expenses can positively affect financial health and stability.

Fixed vs. Variable Expense Management

Managing expenses involves addressing both fixed and variable costs, each with unique characteristics. **Fixed expenses** stay constant regardless of sales or production levels, making them predictable but potentially burdensome if sales decline. These include rent, insurance, and administrative salaries.

On the other hand, **variable expenses** fluctuate with business activity and are often easier to control in the short term. Common examples include sales commissions, marketing costs, and shipping expenses. Variable expenses align with revenue, so they naturally decrease during slow periods. With both types of expenses, consistent monitoring and conscious decision-making can significantly reduce costs and improve profitability.

Strategies and Tactics for Reducing Expenses

Let's explore practical ways to control expenses effectively, whether they're fixed or variable. These strategies are versatile and can be adapted to fit most business types.

Negotiate with Vendors

Negotiating with vendors is one of the quickest ways to cut expenses. Many suppliers offer discounts for bulk orders, early payments, or long-term contracts. Building a solid relationship with vendors also opens doors for exclusive pricing or extended payment terms. For instance, a business could negotiate a 2-5% discount for early payment, which, over time, results in significant savings.

Streamline Administrative Costs

Administrative expenses can quickly add up. Reducing

non-essential activities or combining services can have a noticeable impact on these costs. For example, a business could reduce paper costs by transitioning to digital records.

Cut Marketing Waste

Marketing is essential, but it can often be optimized. Review the return on investment (ROI) of each campaign to identify underperforming ads or strategies. Instead of cutting marketing completely, focus on high-impact channels that drive the most revenue.

Experimenting with digital marketing can often be more cost-effective than traditional methods, such as print or radio advertising.

Improve Utility Usage

Energy, water, and other utilities are necessary but often wasteful expenses. Simple steps, like switching to energy-efficient lighting, reducing peak electricity usage, or even setting up remote work policies to decrease office use, can cut costs. Monitoring utility bills and reducing unnecessary consumption benefits both the business and the environment.

Minimize Waste

Waste reduction is essential, especially for businesses that handle physical products. Streamlining production processes, repurposing by-products, or using recycled materials can save money while supporting sustainability efforts. In office settings, reducing waste can be as simple as going paperless or using eco-friendly supplies.

Reevaluate Subscriptions and Memberships

Many businesses subscribe to multiple software tools or

professional memberships. While valuable, these services can accumulate significant costs over time. Reviewing all subscriptions annually and canceling any that are underused or no longer necessary can help reduce overhead.

Review Insurance Policies

Regularly reviewing insurance policies to ensure the business isn't overpaying for unnecessary coverage can result in savings. It's worthwhile to shop around for new policies or negotiate with existing providers for better rates, particularly if the business has had few claims and improved risk management.

Enforce a Strict Approval Process for Spending

Implementing a strict approval process for significant expenses ensures accountability and reduces impulse spending. Establishing guidelines on which expenses require managerial approval adds a layer of scrutiny to prevent overspending. It also helps employees understand the importance of financial discipline.

A Story of Expense Control: Learning to "Sit on Your Checkbook"

Consider the story of a young man who ran a small construction company. Due to personal issues, he had neglected the business for a while, and it began running at a loss. The business, once a source of pride, now represented uncertainty, and his livelihood was on the line. He was at his wits' end, unsure how to cut costs enough to survive. One day, his wise father visited the business. Seeing the worry etched on his son's face, he encouraged him to share his struggles.

After listening empathetically, the father offered some

hard-earned advice: "Son, I raised you with integrity, and you've always done honest business. But if you want to survive, you need to learn to 'sit on your checkbook.'" Letting that sink in, he continued, "Whenever you need to write a check, don't rush. First, ask yourself if the business will shut down at once if you don't pay that check today. If not, wait another day. And before you sign it, ask for a discount, better prices, or improved payment terms."

The young man, worried about legal repercussions, admitted, "But, Dad, I'm afraid of lawsuits or damaging relationships." The old man reassured him, saying, "These things don't happen overnight, and they don't happen if you keep communicating. Every day you postpone a payment can help you improve your situation. Use that time wisely to cut every single unnecessary expense. And I mean every single one.

You'll be amazed at how things turn around." Before saying goodbye, the old man shared a supporting thought, "I know this will be uncomfortable for a while, but giving up and going out of business will be a lot worse":

Following his father's advice, the young man began scrutinizing each expense. He negotiated with suppliers, reduced waste, and carefully managed his cash flow. It was uncomfortable at first, but he soon saw the difference. His expenses decreased, his cash flow improved, and the business started moving out of the red. His father's advice—to focus on financial discipline and "sit on his checkbook"—was the key to turning things around and ultimately saving his business.

In Summary

Expense control is about discipline, strategy, and persistence. By understanding the unique impact of fixed and variable expenses, adopting practical cost-reduction strategies, and practicing financial restraint, any business can improve its profitability. Whether it's negotiating with vendors, reducing waste, or carefully managing cash flow, each small step adds up. With the right approach, expense control can drive positive change and increase resilience in challenging times.

Using Technology to Decrease Expenses

Technology has transformed the way businesses operate, providing tools and systems to streamline processes, enhance productivity, and reduce costs. Broadly speaking, technology includes the use of systems, devices, applications, and digital tools that improve efficiency in various business functions. For small businesses, technology can be an affordable and effective way to control expenses by optimizing operations.

Below, we explore three major avenues where technology can help reduce expenses: outsourcing, automation, and artificial intelligence (AI).

Outsourcing

Outsourcing is the practice of hiring third-party service providers to handle tasks or functions that would otherwise be performed internally. For small businesses, outsourcing is highly suitable, as it allows them to access specialized skills and resources without incurring the expenses associated with hiring full-time employees. By outsourcing non-core tasks, small businesses can reduce labor costs, focus on critical competencies, and increase operational flexibility.

Example 1: Administrative Outsourcing

One common area for outsourcing is administrative support, such as bookkeeping, payroll processing, or customer service. By outsourcing these tasks, a business can avoid the costs of hiring and training in-house staff, as well as the expenses related to employee benefits and office space.

Example 2: Manufacturing Outsourcing

In manufacturing, outsourcing certain production processes or components can save significant costs. For example, a small business that produces consumer goods might outsource the assembly or packaging of its products to a third-party company. This approach not only reduces in-house labor and equipment costs but also allows the business to focus on other essential areas, like product development and marketing.

Automation

Automation refers to using technology to perform tasks with minimal human intervention. Automation can help small businesses reduce labor costs, improve accuracy, and save time, making it particularly suitable for repetitive or time-consuming tasks.

Automated systems and tools allow small businesses to run efficiently without relying heavily on manual labor, which can lead to considerable cost savings.

Example 1: Administrative Automation

Data entry and document management are common areas for automation in small businesses. Automated software can handle tasks like invoice processing, expense tracking, and report generation, reducing the need for manual work.

Example 2: Manufacturing Automation

In manufacturing, automation can be implemented to streamline production processes. For instance, a small business might invest in automated machinery to handle product sorting, packaging, or assembly. While there may be an initial investment, the long-term savings from reduced labor costs and increased production efficiency often outweigh these costs. Automated production lines can significantly increase output while reducing errors, helping the business achieve consistent quality at a lower expense.

Artificial Intelligence (AI)

AI represents a more advanced level of technology that combines data analysis, machine learning, and predictive capabilities. AI can be integrated into both outsourcing and automation to enhance efficiency further and reduce costs. For small businesses, AI might seem complex or costly, but various accessible tools and applications are making it increasingly viable, even on smaller budgets. AI offers predictive capabilities, allowing businesses to make data-driven decisions, forecast demand, and automate more complex tasks.

How AI Fits into Outsourcing and Automation

AI can enhance the effectiveness of outsourcing by providing tools that support virtual teams or improve remote workflows. For instance, AI-driven chatbots can handle customer inquiries and direct clients to the appropriate service channels, reducing the need for a large customer support team. Similarly, AI tools can assist outsourced bookkeeping teams in detecting financial discrepancies and managing large data sets with greater accuracy and speed.

AI can bring additional precision and adaptability to automation. For administrative tasks, AI-driven software can automate complex tasks like data analysis, trend forecasting, and content generation. For example, AI-based tools can analyze patterns in customer behavior to provide insights into purchasing trends, helping businesses adjust their inventory and marketing strategies more effectively.

In manufacturing, AI-powered machines can analyze and adjust production processes in real time, reducing waste and optimizing resource usage. For instance, predictive maintenance systems use AI to monitor equipment health, alerting operators to potential issues before they result in costly downtime. This approach not only extends the lifespan of equipment but also reduces repair expenses, lowering overall production costs.

Conclusion

Leveraging technology in the form of outsourcing, automation, and artificial intelligence is an effective strategy for small businesses aiming to control expenses and improve profitability. By carefully choosing and implementing these technologies, small businesses can reduce expenses without compromising on quality or service, leading to a more sustainable and profitable operation.

Balancing Investment and Expense Reduction

In managing expenses, business owners face a recurring dilemma: when to cut costs and when to invest in growth. This balance is crucial for long-term success, especially when distinguishing between two primary types of spending: **capital expenditure**

(Capex) and **operational expenditure** (OpEx).

Capital expenditure (Capex) refers to investments made in long-term assets, such as equipment, technology, property, or infrastructure, that benefit the business over several years. These assets are recorded on the balance sheet and depreciated over time, representing a long-term commitment to growth and stability.

In contrast, **operational expenditure (OpEx)**—which we'll simply refer to as "expenses" in this book—covers the day-to-day costs necessary to keep the business running, like rent, salaries, utilities, and marketing. These are short-term expenses, recorded as they occur and directly subtracted from revenue on the income statement. While Capex aims to strengthen the business's future capacity, expenses focus on sustaining current operations.

Balancing Capex and OpEx is vital, as overspending on either can threaten financial stability. Capex investments can improve efficiency, productivity, and scalability, but they require upfront capital. On the other hand, focusing exclusively on reducing expenses might improve short-term profitability but can undermine future growth.

A strategic approach to balancing Capex and OpEx can help small businesses maintain financial health and stay competitive over the long term.

When to Prioritize Expense Reduction Over Capex

In certain circumstances, prioritizing expense reduction and putting Capex on hold is essential for the business's survival. Small businesses operating on tight cash flow or facing immediate financial challenges should focus on reducing expenses. Capex should take a back seat in the following scenarios:

Low Cash Flow or Cash Reserves

When cash flow is tight, the business's immediate focus should be on managing operational expenses to keep daily activities running. Making large investments in assets when cash flow is limited can lead to cash shortages and operational disruptions.

High Debt Levels

When a business carries significant debt, Capex can put a financial strain on it due to additional interest payments. Reducing debt levels before committing to long-term investments can prevent cash flow issues and ensure financial stability.

Economic Uncertainty

In periods of economic downturn or market uncertainty, businesses are often better served by conserving cash. Investing in assets during these times can be risky if revenue declines are possible. A conservative approach to Capex during uncertain times allows the business to remain flexible and prepared to adapt.

Negative or Low-Profit Margins

If profit margins are low, Capex might not be sustainable. Businesses with narrow profit margins should focus on reducing costs, improving efficiency, and increasing profitability before committing to long-term investments.

Unproven Demand or Market Changes

Capex decisions are often based on future growth projections. However, if demand, market trends, or product viability are uncertain, holding off on Capex can protect the business from potential losses.

By prioritizing expense control when facing these challenges, businesses can maintain financial stability and avoid overcommitting resources. Once profitability and cash flow improve, reinvestment through Capex becomes a more viable option.

Balancing Capex and OpEx for Sustainable Growth

Balancing Capex and OpEx requires a strategic approach, as overinvesting in Capex can limit cash for day-to-day operations, while excessive cost-cutting can stifle future growth. Here are practical ways to achieve a healthy balance:

Set Clear Financial Priorities

Begin by identifying the business's immediate financial needs versus its long-term goals. By categorizing expenses based on priority, it's easier to decide where resources should go first. For example, if the primary goal is to improve customer satisfaction, prioritizing investments in customer service technology might take precedence over reducing marketing spend.

Use Financial Ratios for Guidance

Ratios such as the current ratio (current assets divided by current liabilities) and debt-to-equity ratio can help assess whether the business can afford Capex. A healthy current ratio indicates sufficient liquidity, while a manageable debt-to-equity ratio implies the business is not overleveraged. These ratios provide insights into the financial feasibility of Capex decisions.

Assess the ROI of Capex Investments

Each Capex project should be evaluated for its potential return on investment (ROI). If a project has a high potential ROI and aligns with strategic goals, it might justify the expenditure even during tight financial times. For example, purchasing automation equipment to reduce labor costs may have a favorable ROI if it can yield long-term savings and increase productivity.

Leverage Financing Options

When cash flow is limited, financing options such as leases, loans, or grants can make Capex more affordable. Leasing equipment instead of purchasing it outright can reduce upfront costs while allowing the business to access needed assets. However, it's essential to evaluate the terms carefully to avoid excessive interest payments that could strain cash flow.

Phase Investments Over Time

For businesses with constrained budgets, phasing Capex investments can be a practical solution. Rather than committing all resources at once, break large investments into smaller stages. This phased approach spreads costs over time, reducing the immediate financial impact while still allowing the business to benefit from gradual improvements.

Involve the Team in Expense Control

Effective cost management requires a team effort. Encourage employees to find cost-saving opportunities, whether by suggesting more efficient processes or identifying areas of waste. When everyone in the organization contributes to expense control, it becomes easier to reduce OpEx without significantly impacting operations.

By carefully managing both Capex and OpEx, businesses can sustain growth and profitability. Striking this balance requires an understanding of the business's financial position, a focus on high-impact investments, and a commitment to cost control.

Chapter Recap

Chapter 4 focuses on the essential role of expense management in achieving profitability. We began by distinguishing between fixed and variable expenses—those costs outside the Cost of Goods Sold (COGS) that must be covered by gross profit (GP). Fixed expenses, such as rent and salaries, remain constant regardless of sales, while variable expenses fluctuate with production or sales, including items like sales commissions and shipping. Understanding this difference is crucial, as each impacts cash flow and breakeven points differently.

The chapter introduced breakeven analysis as a vital tool for financial stability. Breakeven defines the sales level required to cover all expenses, allowing business owners to understand the revenue needed to avoid losses. We explored two breakeven calculation methods: one for businesses with only fixed expenses and another for those with both fixed and variable costs. Managing expenses can lower breakeven and increase net profit (NP), a concept further supported by exercises in the accompanying Excel workbook.

To control expenses, we discussed practical strategies like negotiating with vendors, optimizing utility usage, and streamlining administrative costs. Through a compelling story, we emphasized the importance of scrutinizing each cost and practicing financial discipline. Finally, we examined the role of technology in expense management, focusing on outsourcing, automation, and AI as cost-effective tools.

Balancing expense reduction with capital investment (Capex) ensures that businesses can grow sustainably while controlling costs. This chapter provides a comprehensive approach to managing expenses, equipping readers with the insights needed to maximize profitability.

This chapter focused on the third of the three keys, namely operating expenses.

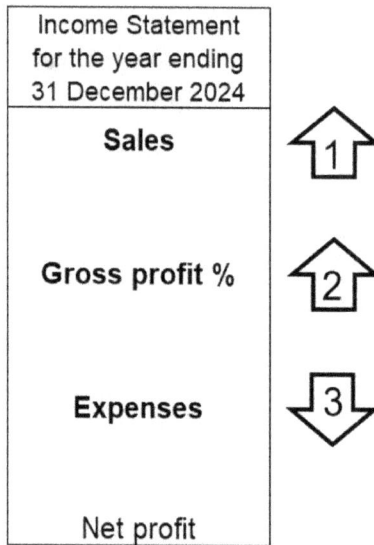

Image 4.1: Reducing expenses for profitability.

Action Plan

Understand Your Expenses: Differentiate between fixed and variable expenses. Track each carefully to know where your money is going and how costs fluctuate with sales.

Use Breakeven Analysis: Calculate your breakeven point to know the minimum sales required to cover expenses. Regularly test scenarios using the provided Excel model to see how changes in expenses or sales impact profitability.

Control Costs: Implement the strategies and tactics for reducing expenses discussed in this chapter.

Leverage Technology: Investigate automation options for repetitive tasks and explore AI tools for insights that can enhance efficiency.

Balance Investments with Expense Reduction: Prioritize high-ROI investments and maintain strict control over operational expenses, especially during uncertain periods.

Chapter 5

Integrating the Three Keys

"Profitability comes from loyalty, productivity, and having a character that attracts people who value what you offer"

– Ziad K Abdelnour

Overview

In the preceding chapters, we examined each of the three essential keys to profitability: Sales, Gross Profit Percentage (GP%), and Expenses. This chapter focuses on how these keys work together, amplifying their impact when strategically integrated. Although they can be managed as separate elements, understanding their interdependence creates a framework that drives exponential profitability and growth.

When sales increase, GP% and expense management play a crucial role in translating that growth into sustainable profits. Conversely, improvements in GP% or reductions in expenses can amplify the effects of sales growth, ensuring that increased revenue contributes more effectively to the bottom line. This synergy reveals a "trickle effect" that, when carefully managed, can significantly impact overall profitability.

In this chapter, we will explore how to set realistic, targeted goals that encompass all three keys. Monitoring performance across these areas helps identify where adjustments may be necessary to maximize profitability. By integrating these keys, you can create a cohesive, practical approach to sustaining and enhancing profitability.

The Interdependence of the 3 Keys

The three keys to profitability—Sales, Gross Profit Percentage (GP%), and Expenses—are interdependent. While each key contributes individually to profit, their combined effects can create a powerful, compounding impact on a business's Net Profit (NP). By understanding how these elements interact, business owners can make informed decisions to maximize their profit potential. When these three keys work in harmony, the cumulative effect on NP goes beyond simple addition; it can lead to exponential growth. This section will explore both the linear and exponential effects that these three elements can have on NP.

An improvement in one of these keys, while the other two remain unchanged, has a straightforward, linear effect on NP. Let's begin by examining the scenario where sales increase while GP% and expenses stay constant. In this case, the additional sales lead to a direct increase in NP. Since GP% stays the same, each additional sale contributes proportionally to profit at a steady rate.

This increase is linear because there is a predictable, one-to-one relationship between the rise in sales and the increase in NP. The added revenue contributes to profit at the established GP% so that NP will grow in direct proportion to the sales increase.

The same linear effect applies when only one of the three keys improves while the others stay the same. For instance, if GP% rises but sales volume and expenses are constant, each sale generates a higher margin, leading to a steady, linear increase in NP. Similarly, if expenses decrease while sales and GP% remain constant, the reduction in costs directly improves NP in a linear way.

In each of these cases, the improvement in NP is purely monetary, and the growth follows a linear path because only one factor is changing. The result is a predictable, steady improvement in NP, making it easy to calculate the impact of each key in isolation.

Understanding the difference between linear and exponential growth is essential in analyzing how the three keys affect NP. **Linear growth** occurs when a change in one variable leads to a proportional, consistent change in another. This one-to-one relationship creates a straight-line effect on a graph, representing steady growth that mirrors the original increase.

In contrast, **exponential growth** involves a multiplying effect, where changes in multiple variables lead to accelerated growth in NP. When two or more of the keys—sales, GP%, and expenses—improve simultaneously, the result on NP is more than the sum of the individual improvements. For instance, if both sales and GP% increase, the added revenue from higher sales is now being multiplied by a larger GP%. This combined effect creates a multiplying, or exponential, impact on NP, as each new sale adds more profit than before.

Now, consider what happens when all three keys improve. With an increase in sales, a higher GP%, and reduced expenses, NP doesn't just grow—it surges. Each sale now contributes more to profit, while the overall expenses decrease, freeing up even more revenue to flow to NP.

This scenario creates an even more exponential effect, where the combined improvements drive profit growth at an accelerating rate. The trickle effect becomes increasingly powerful, and NP can increase dramatically, even with small improvements in each area.

To illustrate the exponential effect, let's assume a business with annual sales of $500,000, a Gross Profit Percentage (GP%) of 40%, and operating expenses totaling $150,000. This results in a Net Profit (NP) of $50,000:

Sales: $500,000

Gross Profit Percentage (GP%): 40%

Gross Profit (GP): $200,000

Expenses: $150,000

Net Profit (NP): $50,000

Now, let's see what happens with a 1% improvement in each of the three keys: sales, GP%, and expenses.

Step 1: 1% Increase in Sales

If sales increase by 1%, they rise from $500,000 to $505,000. With a GP% of 40%, this results in an additional $2,000 in GP (1% of $500,000 x 40%), leading to a new NP of **$52,000**.

Step 2: 1% Increase in GP%

Now, let's increase the GP% by 1%—from 40% to 40.4%. With sales now at $505,000, a GP% of 40.4% results in a GP of $204,020 ($505,000 x 40.4%). After subtracting expenses of $150,000, NP increases to **$54,020**.

Step 3: 1% Decrease in Expenses

Finally, let's reduce expenses by 1%, from $150,000 to $148,500. With a GP of $204,020 and new expenses of $148,500, the NP increases further to **$55,520**.

Result: Compounded Improvement

With each key improved by just 1%, the NP has grown from

$50,000 to $55,520—a total increase of **$5,520**, or **11%**.

This example highlights how even minor, coordinated improvements across the three keys—sales, GP%, and expenses—create a compounding, exponential impact on NP.

(i) To see this effect in action, refer to the Excel worksheet "Gross profit, markup and breakeven" in Appendix B: Resources. Under the tab "Improving NP," this model demonstrates how incremental improvements in each key can compound to produce a greater-than-expected increase in NP. By adjusting sales, GP%, and expenses within the worksheet, readers can visualize the exponential growth effect and explore how small improvements in each area can lead to significant gains in profitability.

Strategy for Simultaneous Improvement

Net Profit (NP) is the lifeblood of any business. It is the ultimate financial goal and the means through which business owners achieve financial growth and security.

For small business owners and corporate executives alike, NP is the term that anchors financial discussions in boardrooms, management meetings, and strategic reviews.

Phrases like "we have to improve the bottom line," "driving NP growth," "maximizing shareholder value through NP," and "enhancing financial performance" are common refrains in corporate environments. The desire to increase NP stems from its vital role in sustaining business health, rewarding stakeholders, and supporting reinvestment.

However, instead of setting a blanket goal around NP improvement, I propose a more strategic approach—one that targets each of the three keys to profitability: Sales, Gross Profit Percentage (GP%), and Expenses. By setting individual goals for each of these keys, a business gains a clearer, more manageable path toward achieving overall profit growth. This approach offers several unique advantages that can transform how a business plans, executes, and checks financial improvements.

Advantages of Targeting the Three Keys

Focused and Realistic Planning

When the focus is shifted from NP alone to each of the three keys, planning becomes more focused and realistic. Setting a goal specifically for one key—whether it's increasing sales, raising GP%, or reducing expenses—allows for a more targeted approach to problem-solving and innovation. Each goal can be clearly defined and aligned with a realistic path for improvement. For instance, a goal to increase GP% might involve negotiating better terms with suppliers, while an expense reduction goal might focus on streamlining administrative costs. This focused approach often yields more practical and achievable goals than a vague mandate to "improve NP."

With each key analyzed independently, the team can set goals that are achievable and tailored to the business's unique circumstances. This approach mitigates the risk of setting overly ambitious or vague goals for NP that may be difficult to reach without specific direction. A well-defined focus on each key also means that the team can address the nuances within each area, such as varying cost structures or sales dynamics, allowing for more tailored, actionable plans.

Increased Engagement and Ownership from Functional Managers

Focusing on one key at a time facilitates active involvement from functional managers who are directly responsible for these areas. When setting a sales goal, the marketing and sales teams are at the forefront of discussions, with a clear mandate to drive growth through specific actions. Likewise, when setting a GP% goal, managers in charge of production, procurement, or service delivery can weigh in on strategies that could increase profitability by improving the costs of goods sold (COGS). Expense-related goals draw in finance, operations, and administrative managers to identify areas where savings can be achieved.

By involving functional managers in each of these targeted discussions, the business fosters a culture of accountability and ownership. Each manager becomes not only responsible for reaching their specific goal but also invested in the overall profitability of the company. This leads to a more engaged management team, where each person understands their role in achieving the company's financial goals. Furthermore, this involvement paves the way for smoother execution of strategies, as managers are more likely to implement plans that they had a hand in developing.

Easier Monitoring and Clearer Insights

Tracking improvements become more straightforward and more transparent when each of the three keys is targeted individually. If a business solely monitors NP, it can be challenging to pinpoint which specific areas contributed to growth or where underperformance may have occurred. A decline in NP might raise questions, but without clear metrics tied to each key, it's difficult to figure out if the issue lies in sales, GP%, or expenses.

In contrast, when the three keys are monitored individually, the business gains precise insights into performance across each area. For instance, if sales increase while GP% or expenses remain unchanged, it becomes clear that the revenue boost is driving NP growth. Similarly, tracking improvements in GP% or expense reductions separately allows the business to identify the specific impact of these efforts. This clarity in monitoring enables quicker adjustments and a more accurate assessment of which strategies are working, fostering an initiative-taking approach to financial management.

Broad Employee Involvement and Buy-In

Engaging a broad range of employees in setting and achieving goals for each key fosters a sense of involvement and teamwork across the organization. Instead of limiting sales goals to the sales or marketing team, involving the entire department brings diverse perspectives, ideas, and insights to the table. Similarly, when setting goals to improve GP%, employees who directly affect COGS—such as production staff, procurement teams, or service workers—should be part of the conversation. Their firsthand experience can reveal opportunities for efficiency improvements that may not be immediately obvious to management alone.

The same principle applies to expense reduction goals. Rather than relying solely on finance or operations managers, involving various departments can uncover hidden costs or inefficiencies. Junior personnel, in particular, may offer fresh perspectives and contribute ideas for streamlining processes or eliminating waste. This company-wide involvement has the added benefit of boosting morale and fostering a sense of shared purpose. Employees who feel they are contributing directly to the company's financial health are more likely to feel motivated and valued, which can enhance overall productivity and job satisfaction.

A Holistic View of Profitability Improvement

Targeting the three keys rather than NP alone creates a holistic view of profitability improvement. NP is the result of various activities and decisions, and by focusing on the individual components—sales, GP%, and expenses—a business can build a more comprehensive strategy. Each key supports the others: higher sales drive revenue, improved GP% enhances margins, and controlled expenses ensure that profits are retained. By addressing each of these areas in tandem, the business builds a solid foundation for sustainable growth.

Focusing on these keys also encourages innovation and creative problem-solving within each area. This integrated approach promotes resilience and adaptability, allowing the business to respond to changing market conditions with agility.

Flexibility and Adaptability in Goal Adjustment

Another advantage of focusing on the three keys is the flexibility it offers in adjusting goals. Economic conditions, industry shifts, or internal changes can affect business performance. When NP alone is the primary focus, adjusting goals can feel challenging and reactive. However, with individual targets for sales, GP%, and expenses, the business has more leeway to adapt its approach.

For example, if market conditions lead to a dip in sales, the business can pivot to focus more on GP% or expense reduction to offset the impact. This flexibility allows for quicker responses to challenges, helping the business stay on track toward profitability even when conditions change.

Adjustments to each key can be made independently, giving managers the ability to focus on areas with the most immediate potential for improvement.

Using NP as a Benchmark, Not the Primary Goal

While NP remains a critical metric, it serves best as a benchmark rather than the primary goal in this approach. The NP Improvement Model in the Excel spreadsheet (found in Appendix B: Resources) offers a tool to predict the impact of changes in each key on the overall NP.

By inputting potential improvements in sales, GP%, and expenses, business owners can estimate the resulting NP and adjust their strategies accordingly. This allows for a realistic forecast of NP growth while maintaining the primary focus on the three keys.

By shifting the focus from NP to the three keys, business owners gain a more actionable, transparent, and adaptable framework for driving profitability. With targeted goals, employee engagement, and clear tracking, the business can achieve sustainable growth while fostering a culture of collaboration and continuous improvement.

Monitor and Adjust

To ensure that each of the three keys—Sales, GP%, and Expenses—consistently supports the business's profitability goals, establishing a structured approach to monitoring and adjusting is essential.

Tracking progress doesn't just mean checking numbers; it's about creating a framework that keeps goals within reach while maintaining agility to respond to changing conditions. A proactive and disciplined approach will help the business stay on course and make necessary changes to maximize profit.

Regular Review

The first and most crucial step in effective monitoring is to set up a regular review cycle. By setting fixed intervals to review performance, the business can catch issues early and make prompt adjustments. While review cycles can vary, aiming for the shortest possible cycle is generally best. Monthly reviews provide an optimal balance: they allow for enough time to see the effects of changes but are short enough to keep decision-making responsive. Monthly reviews enable the business to detect trends in Sales, GP%, or Expenses before they become too costly to fix. For example, a drop in GP% due to supplier cost increases can be addressed quickly, avoiding prolonged profit erosion.

Longer cycles, such as quarterly or semi-annual reviews, carry risks. If issues arise at the start of a quarter or six-month period, they may go unnoticed until the next review. For example, a sudden spike in expenses left unchecked for half a year can drain resources, while a promising sales opportunity could be missed if not addressed promptly. Monthly reviews provide the regular feedback necessary to adjust strategies and stay aligned with profit goals, minimizing the chance of small problems snowballing into significant setbacks.

Quick Response

A regular review cycle alone is not enough; it must be coupled with a commitment to quick responses when issues are identified. Once any deviation from goals is noticed, it's essential to analyze the cause and act without delay. If sales underperform compared to the target, determine potential factors—such as shifts in market demand or increased competition—and explore strategies to address the gap. Quick responses may involve adjusting marketing tactics, revisiting sales strategies, or revising pricing temporarily to stimulate demand.

Similarly, if GP% is lower than projected, assess internal and external factors affecting profitability. Expense fluctuations also demand immediate attention, whether they stem from rising energy costs, administrative overhead, or unexpected expenses. Acting fast to control these variances helps ensure they don't grow into significant, lasting issues that could jeopardize profitability.

Continuous Improvement

Monitoring and adjusting shouldn't be limited to fixing issues when they arise. Adopting a continuous improvement mindset allows the business to leverage each review cycle as an opportunity to build resilience and enhance profitability over time.

Even if the current goals are met, ask whether there is potential for further improvement. Is there an area in Sales that could benefit from an innovative approach or a partnership to expand reach? Could GP% be increased by finding alternative suppliers or refining product quality to attract higher-value clients? Are there still areas in Expenses that could be streamlined or even outsourced for better efficiency?

Continuous improvement also involves seeking feedback from all levels of the organization. Team members involved in Sales, GP%, and expense management often have valuable insights that may lead to innovative solutions or reveal new opportunities for efficiency. Encouraging this mindset not only improves profitability but also fosters a culture of shared responsibility and forward-thinking among employees.

In summary, effective monitoring and adjustment of the three keys require a proactive approach. A short review cycle, ideally monthly, allows for prompt adjustments and keeps the business agile. Responding quickly to deviations ensures that minor problems are corrected before they grow, while a focus on continuous improvement drives sustainable growth and fosters resilience.

Chapter Recap

In Chapter 5, we explored how integrating the three keys to profitability—Sales, Gross Profit Percentage (GP%), and Expenses—can create a compounding effect on Net Profit (NP).

Each key can influence NP individually, but when managed in tandem, their combined impact can drive exponential growth. We discussed that while increasing any one of these keys produces a linear increase in NP, simultaneous improvements across all three lead to more significant, exponential gains.

By targeting each key individually, a business gains more actionable, transparent goals and involves relevant team members across functions, from sales to procurement to expense management. This approach promotes focused planning, where each area can be addressed independently, yielding more precise and more realistic goals that involve the whole organization. By doing so, companies can enhance engagement and establish a structured approach to monitoring and adjusting each key for continuous improvement.

In closing, we emphasized the importance of a proactive review cycle—ideally monthly—to allow quick responses to deviations, with continuous improvement at the forefront. These structured steps empower the business to sustain and grow profitability over time by aligning individual goals within a cohesive, strategic framework.

Action Plan

Engage Your Team: Involve team members directly in goal-setting and problem-solving. For example, include production staff in discussions about GP% improvements and administrative teams in expense reviews.

Set Targeted Goals: Define specific, realistic targets for each key—Sales, GP%, and Expenses. Use the SMART principle (Specific, Measurable, Achievable, Relevant, Time-bound).

Establish Monthly Reviews: Schedule monthly reviews to check progress on each key. This frequency allows you to catch trends early.

Act Quickly on Deviations: When performance slips, analyze the cause and respond promptly with focused actions.

Pursue Continuous Improvement: Treat every review as a chance to refine your strategies. Even when goals are met, seek new efficiencies or opportunities for growth.

Chapter 6
Financial Tools and Techniques for Profitability

"Chasing money is the surest way to failure. Focus on delivering value, and profit will follow" – Oprah Winfrey

Overview

In this chapter, we delve into essential financial strategies and metrics that help small business owners drive their profitability. The chapter begins by examining three key profit metrics—Net Profit, Operating Profit (EBIT), and EBITDA. Each metric offers unique insights, with Net Profit providing a comprehensive view, Operating Profit focusing on core operational efficiency, and EBITDA stripping out non-cash expenses to reveal cash-generating ability. Together, these metrics give business owners a multi-dimensional understanding of profitability.

We then explore the power of financial statements, particularly the income statement, balance sheet, and cash flow statement, as tools for decision-making. Utilizing graphs and trendlines helps visualize financial progress, making it easier to spot trends and identify opportunities for improvement. Cash flow management emerges as a vital focus, where balancing inflows and outflows ensures both liquidity and profitability. Strategies include optimizing inventory levels, incentivizing prompt payments, and carefully timing expenses.

Finally, the chapter introduces a practical approach by integrating forecasting, budgeting, and cash flow projections into a unified 3-in-1 financial planning tool. This approach, tailored for small businesses, combines long-term strategy with day-to-day financial control, providing a cohesive view of finances in one document. Overall, this chapter equips small business owners with actionable tools to enhance financial clarity, discipline, and adaptability, fostering sustainable growth.

Different Profit Metrics

To this point, we've focused on maximizing net profit by managing three essential keys: sales, gross profit, and expenses. Now, to gain a fuller understanding, we'll explore three popular profit metrics: **Net Profit**, **Operating Profit (EBIT)**, and **EBITDA**.

These metrics help illustrate a business's profitability from various perspectives, each one offering unique insights into financial performance. By understanding them, business owners can better analyze their finances and make well-informed decisions about growth and profitability.

Net Profit

Net profit is the "bottom line" in any business. It represents the final accounting profit after all expenses have been deducted. The calculation is simple:

Net Profit = Sales – Expenses

In more formal accounting terms, the formula can also be expressed as:

Net Income = Revenue – Expenses

This profit metric is widely used because it shows the actual earnings left over after covering all costs. It reflects the total earnings available to owners and shareholders or for reinvestment in the business.

Net profit is considered an *accounting profit* because it relies on accrual accounting. In accrual accounting, revenue and expenses are recognized when they are earned or incurred, not necessarily when cash is received or paid.

This approach differs from cash-based accounting, where transactions are recorded only when money changes hands. Accrual accounting is required by both Generally Accepted Accounting Principles (GAAP) and International Financial Reporting Standards (IFRS), and it provides a more comprehensive view of a business's financial health.

Net profit is a straightforward metric for small business owners, as it accounts for all income and costs, including taxes and interest. Monitoring this metric enables business owners to see whether they are operating at a profit or loss, offering a clear view of the company's sustainability. Net profit is also a critical indicator for lenders and investors, as it shows profitability after all obligations are met.

Operating Profit (EBIT)

Operating profit is similar to net profit but excludes interest and taxes, making it a valuable metric for assessing core operational performance. Often referred to as *Earnings Before Interest and Taxes (EBIT)*, operating profit highlights the profit generated by a company's core activities, independent of financial and tax considerations.

The formula is: Operating Profit (EBIT) = Net Profit + Interest +

Taxes

Operating profit is also considered an *accounting profit* because it is based on accrual accounting principles. This metric helps business owners understand how well their primary operations generate profit before financing costs or tax obligations are factored in.

Unlike net profit, operating profit focuses purely on operational efficiency, making it useful for internal management to track the profitability of core business activities.

EBITDA

EBITDA, which stands for *Earnings Before Interest, Taxes, Depreciation, and Amortization*, is another widely used metric for evaluating core profitability. By further excluding depreciation and amortization, EBITDA provides a view of the business's earnings that disregards both financing choices and non-cash accounting expenses. The formula for calculating EBITDA is:

EBITDA = Net Profit + Interest + Taxes + Depreciation + Amortization or

EBITDA = EBIT + Depreciation + Amortization

By focusing on EBITDA, business owners can get a clearer picture of the company's operating profit before the influence of capital structure or asset depreciation. This is valuable because depreciation and amortization are non-cash expenses, meaning they don't represent actual cash outflows.

As a result, EBITDA often provides a more direct view of cash-generating ability, which is particularly useful for comparing profitability across different companies or industries.

EBITDA in Perspective

Although EBITDA can be a helpful indicator of profitability, it's not a standard metric under GAAP or IFRS. Instead, it's a *non-GAAP* measure widely used by analysts, investors, and larger companies to assess core operating performance without the impact of financing or accounting decisions. It's particularly beneficial for comparing companies with different tax rates or debt structures.

However, EBITDA may have limited applicability for small business owners. Small businesses often operate with simpler financial structures, and most don't need complex measures that exclude depreciation, amortization, or other non-operating items. Net profit is usually sufficient to provide a meaningful measure of profitability for these businesses, as it accounts for all income and expenses, including tax and interest.

In this book, we will continue to use the term **Net Profit (NP)** for simplicity. Using NP offers specific advantages for small businesses, including:

Simplicity: Small businesses typically have straightforward financial operations without substantial debt, complex tax arrangements, or significant fixed assets. For many, net profit provides a complete view of their financial health without the need to exclude non-cash or financing elements.

Tax Considerations: Small businesses often have different tax implications compared to large corporations. Focusing on net profit, which includes taxes, provides a more accurate picture of profitability and avoids the complexity of adjusting for tax obligations separately.

In summary, understanding these different profit metrics allows business owners to see profitability from multiple angles. While net profit provides an all-encompassing view, operating profit hones in on core operating efficiency, and EBITDA removes financing and non-cash expenses to assess cash-generating potential.

Figure 6.1 gives a simple illustration of the three metrics.

Income Statement for the year ending 31 December 2024		
Sales	200,000	
less: COGS	120,000	
= **Gross Profit**	80,000	
Gross Profit %	40%	
less: **Expenses**	32,000	
Rent	6,000	
Utilities	2,500	
Shipping costs	3,500	
Office supplies	1,000	
Admin salaries	7,250	
Insurance	2,000	
Marketing	4,000	
Travel expenses	2,750	
Depreciation	3,000	
= **EBIT**	48,000	2
less: Interest	1,500	
less: Tax	2,500	
= **Net Profit (NP)**	44,000	1

EBITDA = NP + Interest + Tax + Depreciation + Amortization
or   EBITDA = EBIT + Depreciation + Amortization
= 48,000 + 3,000 + 0
= 51,000   3

Figure 6.1: Net profit, EBIT, and EBITDA.

For most small business owners, net profit remains by far the most practical and informative metric. It captures all aspects of the business's financial health and is easy to monitor and interpret.

Using Financial Statements to Drive Decisions

A common hurdle for many entrepreneurs and small business owners is a need for business management skills, particularly in financial matters. Studies show that limited financial literacy can be a significant barrier to effective business management. According to the Organisation for Economic Co-operation and Development (OECD), many small business owners and entrepreneurs need more financial skills to make informed business decisions, which can hinder their success. This gap in financial literacy can affect everything from budgeting to financial forecasting, leading to missed opportunities for growth.

This book seeks to address part of this gap by focusing on three critical levers for profitability—sales, gross profit, and expenses—using the income statement as a primary tool. By understanding and managing these levers, small business owners can unlock valuable insights into their business's performance. With the right approach, financial literacy can be developed over time, empowering business owners to make sound financial decisions and improve their company's profitability.

Entrepreneurs can significantly benefit from continuous learning. As they build financial knowledge, they can better manage their resources, make data-driven decisions, and navigate challenges more effectively. Financial literacy isn't just a skill; it's a foundation for sustainable success. Continuous learning equips business owners to interpret financial data, adjust strategies, and ultimately achieve greater business stability.

While we emphasize the income statement in this book, ideally, business owners should consider all major financial statements. The three critical financial statements—the income statement, cash flow statement, and balance sheet—each offer distinct perspectives on a business's financial health. Supporting statements[1] provide further detail and insight, enhancing a business owner's ability to make well-rounded decisions. For simplicity and focus, we will continue to prioritize the income statement in this discussion.

Graphs and Trendlines

One of the most effective techniques for tracking financial progress is using graphs and trendlines. Graphs visually display data, making it easier to see overall performance and compare results across different periods. Trendlines are particularly useful for tracking changes in specific metrics over time, such as sales growth or expense trends.

A trendline on a graph is a smoothed line that illustrates the general direction of a dataset, helping to highlight upward or downward trends. When combined, graphs and trendlines offer a powerful visual summary—providing insights that can be more impactful than rows of numbers. As the saying goes, a picture is worth a thousand words; in this case, a trendline may be worth even more.

Most accounting software today, including basic options, can generate graphs and add trendlines. These features help small business owners visualize data without needing specialized skills or advanced software. If accounting software lacks this feature, creating charts and trendlines in Excel is straightforward. Excel allows users to enter data and quickly transform it into visual

---

1. Statement of Shareholders' Equity (or Statement of Retained Earnings), Notes to Financial Statements, Management's Discussion and Analysis (MD&A), and Financial Statement Footnotes.

summaries with graphs, making it accessible to nearly any business owner.

To illustrate the point, consider Figure 6.2, a dataset for Sales, GP, GP%, Expenses, and NP over 12 months.

Sales	GP	GP%	Expenses	NP
50,000	16,500	33.0%	10,000	6,500
51,000	16,830	33.0%	11,000	5,830
51,250	17,271	33.7%	10,000	7,271
51,500	17,253	33.5%	10,500	6,753
51,250	17,323	33.8%	10,000	7,323
52,000	17,680	34.0%	9,750	7,930
52,200	17,696	33.9%	9,750	7,946
52,000	17,680	34.0%	9,750	7,930
52,500	17,850	34.0%	9,600	8,250
52,750	17,988	34.1%	9,500	8,488
52,700	17,813	33.8%	9,500	8,313
53,000	18,020	34.0%	9,300	8,720

% Increase or Decrease				
+6.00%	+9.21%	+3.03%	-7.00%	+34.15%

Figure 6.2: Example dataset for Sales, GP, GP%, Expenses, and NP.

At a glance, it is merely a block of numbers, not saying much about progress, if any. It is only when we start interpreting the data that the results become clear. For example, compare the block of numbers with the single row of percentages at the bottom. That single row tells a story of overall improvement. Notice the exponential effect on the NP.

Now consider Figures 6.3 and 6.4. The first graph compares the trendlines of GP and GP%, and the second graph displays the movement of Sales, Expenses, and NP.

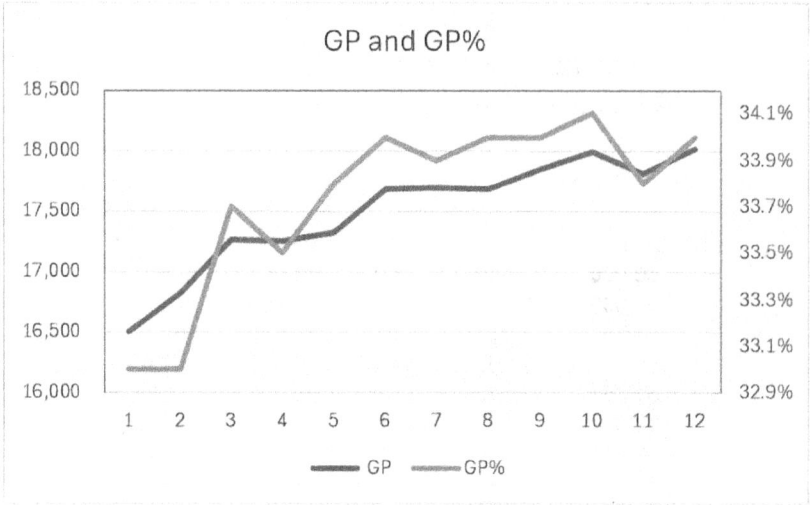

Figure 6.3: Split graph for GP and GP%.

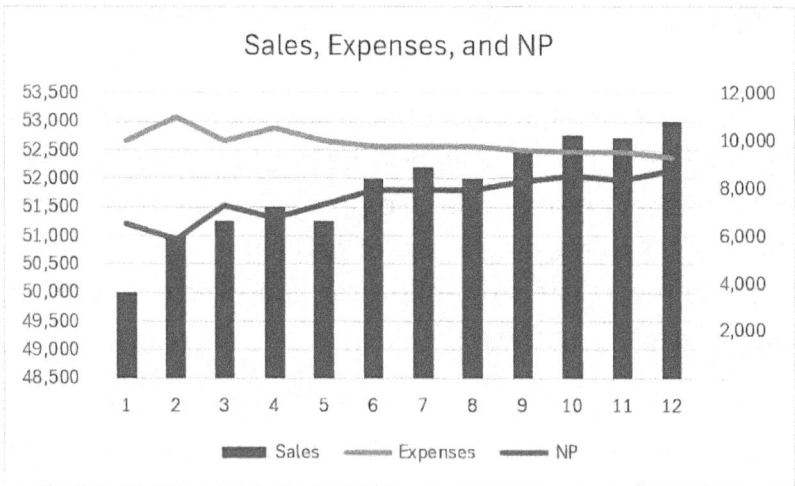

Figure 6.4: Stacked graph for Sales, Expenses, and NP.

By using financial statements and visual tools, entrepreneurs can bridge gaps in financial literacy and make well-informed decisions. Graphs and trendlines simplify complex data, allowing small business owners to quickly understand financial patterns, identify potential issues, and celebrate successes.

Cash Flow Management

Managing cash flow effectively is crucial for small business owners striving for profitability. While achieving a solid net profit is essential, it should never come at the expense of cash flow health. Many profitable businesses still face cash flow problems, which can lead to operational disruptions or, worse, financial instability. To ensure business sustainability, cash flow, and profitability must be balanced, creating a healthy financial foundation. This section will discuss both the inflow and outflow of money and highlight critical areas to check for maintaining strong cash flow.

Sources of Money Flowing In

A steady stream of cash inflows is vital to keeping the business running smoothly. Income can come from multiple sources, each with its cash flow implications. Let's review several primary sources and what to monitor.

Cash Sales vs. Credit Sales

Sales are the primary source of income for most businesses. However, the nature of these sales—whether cash or credit—affects cash flow differently. Cash sales provide immediate funds, which is ideal for covering daily expenses without delay. By contrast, credit sales allow clients to buy now and pay later, which may delay cash inflow. While credit sales can help attract more clients, they introduce a risk of delayed payments or non-payment, potentially straining cash flow.

To strike a balance, small business owners can set up a policy for credit sales, limiting them to clients with a strong payment history. Tracking credit sales as a percentage of total sales is helpful. If credit sales form a substantial part of the business, it's crucial to monitor accounts receivable closely to avoid cash shortages.

Remember: Sales is vanity, profit is sanity, cash is king!

Monitoring Debtors and Aging Accounts

For businesses that offer credit sales, managing debtors—clients who owe money—is essential. When payments are delayed, cash flow suffers, even if sales are strong. One effective tool for monitoring debtors is an aging report, which categorizes accounts receivable by the length of time they've been outstanding. This report shows if payments are overdue, allowing business owners to take prompt action to recover funds.

To encourage prompt payment, consider offering incentives for early settlement. Discounts for early payment can motivate clients to pay sooner, improving cash flow. For example, a 2% discount for payments made within ten days can be beneficial if the cost of waiting for a full payment outweighs the discount.

Consistent follow-up with debtors and clear communication regarding payment terms also support prompt payments and reduce cash flow risks.

Preparing for Cash Shortfalls

Sometimes, cash flow shortfalls are inevitable, especially during seasonal downturns or periods of high investment. When a cash squeeze is expected, having access to credit can be a valuable backup. Standard options include a business overdraft, a business credit card, or a line of credit. Each type of credit has different terms and costs, so choose an option that aligns with the business's cash flow cycle.

Planning for credit access ahead of time prevents cash flow emergencies from turning into crises. It's wise to negotiate favorable terms with financial institutions in advance, ensuring that funds are available when needed. Using credit responsibly and keeping credit costs under control helps manage cash flow without incurring excessive debt.

Additional Sources of Cash Inflow

Aside from sales and credit arrangements, consider alternative sources of cash inflow. For example, leasing out assets that aren't in constant use can generate added income without requiring extra sales. Early invoice payments or advance payments from clients are also options for improving cash flow. Some businesses use invoice factoring, where they sell outstanding invoices to a third party at a discount to access cash sooner. However, the latter should be evaluated carefully, as it comes with high fees and reduced profit margins.

The Outflow of Money and Key Considerations

Monitoring cash outflows is as essential as tracking inflows. By managing expenses effectively, business owners can prevent unnecessary cash shortages. Below are typical outflows and strategies for managing them.

Inventory Levels and Stock Turnover

Excess inventory ties up cash that could be used elsewhere, which is particularly problematic for businesses with high stock levels. Monitoring the stock turnover rate—the speed at which inventory is sold and replaced—can provide insight into cash flow management. A high turnover rate suggests efficient inventory use, while a low turnover rate may indicate that cash is tied up in unsold stock.

To maintain efficient cash flow, business owners should avoid overstocking and aim to keep inventory at levels that match sales demand. Conducting regular inventory reviews and adjusting stock based on demand forecasts can reduce excess stock and improve cash availability.

Timing of Expense Payments

Timing can significantly affect cash flow. While commendable, paying expenses before their due dates can strain cash reserves. Many suppliers offer net terms, allowing for delayed payments. By adhering to these terms, businesses can keep cash in hand for as long as possible, optimizing cash flow without risking late fees.

In cases where suppliers offer discounts for early payment, evaluate if the discount is worth taking. For instance, a 2% discount for paying within ten days (commonly expressed as 2/10, net 30) can be helpful if the business has sufficient cash flow and if the discount outweighs potential interest earned by holding the cash longer.

Payment Terms with Creditors

In addition to managing the timing of expenses, small business owners should work to negotiate favorable payment terms with creditors. Extending payment terms by even a few days can help maintain cash reserves for operational needs. Regularly reviewing creditor terms and requesting extensions, when possible, can create breathing room in cash flow. Building a good relationship with suppliers may also open opportunities for flexible payment options during difficult periods.

Calculating the Benefit of Early Settlement Discounts

When creditors offer an early settlement discount, it's essential to determine whether it is cost-effective.

To calculate, compare the discount amount with the benefit of using cash for other purposes. For example, if a supplier offers a discount for paying within ten days, this could be a desirable choice if the business has a positive cash balance and the cost savings from the discount are higher than the potential return from holding the cash.

The formula to evaluate if an early settlement discount is worthwhile is:

Discount Savings > Return from Holding Cash

On the other side, when a business is in overdraft, it's beneficial to take the early payment discount only if the discount savings outweigh the interest cost on the overdraft. The decision formula in this case is:

Discount Savings > Interest Cost on Overdraft

These calculations allow business owners to make data-driven decisions that benefit cash flow while considering opportunity costs.

Other Cash Outflows to Monitor

Besides inventory and creditor payments, there are other outflows to watch closely. Payroll is a significant expense for most businesses, and managing it well is crucial. Some companies may align payroll schedules with cash inflows to ensure smoother cash flow.

Additionally, reviewing utility bills, insurance premiums, and maintenance costs for efficiency can reduce cash outflows.

Seasonal expenses, such as marketing costs for peak seasons, should also be planned well in advance. By setting aside funds during high-cash-flow periods, business owners can cover these seasonal outflows without stressing the budget.

In conclusion, cash flow management requires balancing incoming and outgoing funds to sustain business operations and profitability. Monitoring credit sales, incentivizing prompt payments, and preparing for shortfalls can strengthen cash inflow.

On the outflow side, controlling inventory levels, optimizing payment timing, and evaluating early settlement discounts all contribute to healthy cash flow.

With careful planning and regular review, small business owners can maintain a steady cash flow, creating a solid financial foundation for long-term growth.

Forecasting and Budgeting

One of the most powerful steps a business owner can take in managing finances is effective planning. Forecasting, budgeting, and projecting cash flow all bring business goals into focus, offering a practical, simple path to financial clarity and discipline.

This section provides a logical progression through each of these essential planning tools, showing how, when combined, they can create an integrated financial roadmap for small business success.

Forecasting

Definition and Purpose of Forecasting

Forecasting is the process of projecting future financial performance based on past and present data. In a business context, it involves predicting revenues, costs, and profits over a certain period, typically a year. Forecasting helps businesses make informed decisions about resource allocation, cost control, and growth strategies. It serves as a predictive tool, giving a business a foundation to anticipate future needs and opportunities.

Forecasting is imperative because it allows businesses to set realistic targets, allocate resources efficiently, and prepare for fluctuations in income or expenses. For small businesses, an accurate forecast supports proactive management and minimizes the risk of cash shortages or missed growth opportunities.

Components of a Forecast

In financial forecasting, certain income statement items should be projected:

Sales Revenue: Revenue, which reflects the expected income from sales, is the foundation of any forecast. This item is typically broken down by product or service lines, regions, or customer segments.

Gross Profit (GP%): Forecasting gross profit percentage (GP%) determines the spending on COGS and helps businesses understand profitability before accounting for expenses. Gross profit is crucial for setting spending limits and gauging overall financial health.

Expenses: Operating expenses include salaries, marketing, utilities, and other costs that aren't directly tied to COGS.

Forecasting these expenses helps determine how much revenue will cover day-to-day business needs.

Net Profit (NP): The goal of forecasting is to project net profit, which shows the financial outcome after all expenses. Forecasting NP helps businesses plan for growth and ensure that profitability aligns with financial goals.

Budgeting

Definition and Importance of Budgeting

Budgeting is the process of creating a detailed financial plan that outlines a business's revenue, expenses, and net profit over a set period, often a year. Unlike forecasting, which projects what is likely to happen, a budget provides a spending plan that limits expenditures and helps achieve financial targets. Budgeting creates a framework for monitoring performance, offering structure and financial discipline.

Budgets are crucial because they guide spending decisions, ensuring resources are used wisely and aligned with financial goals. They function as a control mechanism, allowing businesses to compare actual outcomes against planned expenses, which supports accountability and encourages cost control.

Components of a Budget

Essential income statement items included in a budget are:

Revenue Targets: Like forecasting, budgeting includes expected sales revenue. However, in budgeting, this revenue is viewed as a target rather than a projection.

Planned COGS: The budget specifies expected COGS, reflecting the cost of materials, labor, and other production expenses tied to revenue targets.

Expenses: Budgeting allocates funds for regular business operations, setting spending limits on items like rent, salaries, utilities, and marketing.

Planned Net Profit: The budget includes a target for net profit, ensuring that financial resources are allocated to meet profitability goals.

Combining Forecasting and Budgeting

It is now clear that forecasting and budgeting have the same elements—revenue, COGS, expenses, and net profit—but differ in purpose. Forecasting is strategic, offering a long-term view that supports planning and decision-making at a high level. It sets broad financial targets that guide the business's direction. In contrast, budgeting is tactical, breaking down these targets into day-to-day operational limits that help control spending and track performance. Given this alignment of components but the difference in focus, combining forecasting and budgeting into a single document is both practical and workable.

This combined approach is designed for small businesses, not for large corporations with expansive accounting departments. In small businesses, time and resources are limited, making a streamlined, practical approach essential. By integrating forecasting and budgeting, small business owners can gain significant insights without adding complexity.

Budgeting's Reliance on Forecasting

Effective budgeting starts with a reasonable forecast. Forecasting provides the baseline projections for revenue and costs, making it possible to allocate resources meaningfully. Without an accurate forecast, a budget is just a guess; with it, the budget becomes a roadmap.

Benefits of a 2-in-1 Planning Approach

Combining forecasting and budgeting allows business owners to project and control finances in a single, cohesive document. This combination offers the flexibility to adapt spending as actuals change, creating a responsive yet disciplined financial plan.

Understanding a Rolling Budget

A rolling budget continuously updates the financial plan based on real-time data. Each month, the budget rolls forward another period, keeping a one-year horizon. This type of budget can be highly effective for businesses in rapidly changing environments, as it provides agility. However, it's worth noting that rolling budgets require regular updates and can lead to frequent changes, which may disrupt planning if not managed carefully.

Benefits and Drawbacks of 2-in-1 Planning

The 2-in-1 approach offers several benefits, including simplified tracking, reduced time spent reconciling separate forecasts and budgets, and improved alignment between expected and planned financial outcomes. However, small business owners should be cautious of over-reliance on projections; too much adjustment can lead to "budget creep," where spending increases slowly over time.

Projected Cash Flow Statement

Before discussing how to combine the above with cash flow, it's essential to clarify what a projected cash flow statement entails. Unlike a formal cash flow statement prepared at the end of an accounting period, a projected cash flow statement is a month-by-month plan that anticipates cash inflows and outflows based on the forecast and budget.

Difference from Formal Cash Flow Statements

The formal cash flow statement, part of the GAAP and IFRS requirements, categorizes cash movements into operating, investing, and financing activities. A projected cash flow statement, however, focuses on cash flow within a shorter time frame, primarily through operating activities, helping small business owners manage daily liquidity needs.

Components of a Monthly Projected Cash Flow

A projected cash flow statement requires these key elements:

Sales and GP%: Projected sales revenue and gross profit percentage determine the expected cash from operations.

Cash Sales Percentage: Estimating the percentage of sales paid in cash versus credit determines the immediate cash inflow from sales.

Debtor Payment Terms: The cash inflow from debtor payments is determined by how long clients take to pay on average.

Cash Purchases Percentage: Estimating what percentage of purchases will be paid in cash versus credit determines the immediate cash outflow from COGS.

Creditor Payment Terms: Understanding the time frame for paying suppliers allows for accurate timing of cash outflows paying creditors.

Expenses: Usually, it is easiest to assume expenses are all paid in cash.

For simplicity, the listed requirements above exclude financing transactions, capital expenditures (CapEx), and taxes. However, these can easily be added if needed for a more comprehensive view.

Combining Forecast, Budget, and Projected Cash Flow

While combining these three planning tools is not typical in corporate finance, it's a practical and powerful tool for small businesses. This 3-in-1 financial document offers an integrated view of income, expenses, and cash flow, ensuring business owners are prepared to meet financial obligations.

Benefits of a 3-in-1 Financial Tool

The combined document is efficient and straightforward, enabling business owners to track and manage finances in one place. It simplifies the planning process, allowing adjustments as needed without over-complicating the financial plan. A 3-in-1 tool offers a holistic view of profitability and liquidity, helping business owners anticipate cash flow gaps and avoid surprises.

Drawbacks to Consider

The main drawback is the need for accurate projections. If initial forecasts are unrealistic, the combined document may provide misleading information, leading to poor decision-making. Additionally, this tool requires regular updates to remain accurate, which can be time-consuming for small business owners.

Implementing the Planning

Most basic accounting software offers the tools necessary to create this 3-in-1 financial document. For businesses with complex needs, advanced software or consulting with financial management experts may be needed.

Small business owners who outsource their accounting can still implement this approach. By requesting a monthly cash flow projection at the start of each period, owners can rely on their service provider's expertise. Alternatively, creating this document in Excel is straightforward and involves an initial setup that can be reused. This planning tool offers a substantial return on the time invested.

Conclusion

Integrating forecasting, budgeting, and projected cash flow into a single document creates a dynamic tool for small business owners. This 3-in-1 approach provides financial clarity, discipline, and adaptability, ensuring a well-rounded view of profitability and cash flow. Through practical planning and regular updates, business owners can achieve stability, growth, and a proactive approach to financial management.

Chapter Recap

In this chapter, we explored essential financial tools and techniques designed to enhance small business profitability. We began by discussing different profit metrics—Net Profit, Operating Profit, and EBITDA—each offering unique insights into a company's financial performance. Understanding these metrics allows business owners to evaluate profitability from multiple angles and make informed decisions.

Next, we examined the use of financial statements as tools for decision-making, focusing on how income statements, cash flow statements, and balance sheets provide critical data. Using graphs and trendlines, we highlighted the value of tracking financial progress visually, making patterns easier to spot.

Cash flow management emerged as a critical component, showing how essential it is to balance profitability with liquidity. We covered strategies for managing inflows and outflows to maintain healthy cash flow, such as optimizing inventory levels, negotiating payment terms, and monitoring debtor aging.

Finally, we introduced the concept of combining forecasting, budgeting, and cash flow projections into a single, practical 3-in-1 planning document. This approach offers a holistic view of a business's financial health, promoting financial clarity, discipline, and adaptability for small business owners.

Action Plan

Understand Your Profit Metrics: Focus on Net Profit, Operating Profit, and EBITDA to assess profitability. Use Net Profit as your primary indicator but understand how the other metrics provide additional insights.

Leverage Financial Statements: Review the income statement and balance sheet regularly (monthly). Use graphs and trendlines to track changes in sales, GP, GP%, and expenses over time.

Manage Cash Flow Actively: Monitor inflows from cash and credit sales and maintain clear debtor terms. Avoid cash shortages by managing inventory, optimizing payment terms, and using credit wisely when needed.

Combine Forecasting, Budgeting, and Cash Flow: Develop a 3-in-1 document that integrates forecasting, budgeting, and cash flow projections. This tool provides a unified view of your finances, helping you adjust quickly to changes.

Chapter 7
Case Studies

"Success is the sum of small efforts, repeated day in and day out" –
Robert Collier

Overview

This chapter presents three compelling case studies that demonstrate the critical interplay between the three keys to profitability. Each case study offers unique insights into strategic decision-making and its consequences, showcasing both successful applications and pitfalls to avoid.

The first case study highlights Celia, a natural body care entrepreneur who successfully expanded her business through agent sales and cost management. Her story emphasizes how calculated risks and innovation can lead to significant growth without expanding physical operations.

The second case study features George, a swimming pool contractor who maximized profitability by introducing premium features and redesigning his product to reduce costs. His journey demonstrates how listening to customer feedback and innovating within constraints can enhance both revenue and efficiency.

The final case study delves into Dave's landscaping business, a cautionary tale about overextending resources and compromising quality in the pursuit of growth. Dave's missteps in underbidding commercial contracts, using cheaper materials, and mismanaging his team underscore the importance of balancing sales volume with sustainable practices.

Together, these case studies provide practical lessons and clear examples of how businesses can strategically manage the three keys to profitability, avoiding common pitfalls while driving sustainable growth.

Case Study 1: Celia's Natural Success Story

Introduction

Celia is a savvy entrepreneur with a passion for natural body care. Her cozy shop in a suburban strip mall and her online store offer high-quality soaps and lotions crafted from natural ingredients. From the outset, she made the strategic decision to outsource manufacturing. This allowed her to avoid the complexities of managing a production facility, such as buying equipment, maintaining large premises, and employing specialized staff. Instead, she partnered with a local contract manufacturer who met her product standards while keeping costs predictable.

With a steady monthly sales volume of $40,000, Celia achieved a gross profit percentage (GP%) of 60%, translating into $24,000 in gross profit. After covering her modest operating expenses, she enjoyed a comfortable net profit.

However, Celia's enterprising spirit drove her to explore ways to grow her business without expanding her shop or introducing new product lines. Her journey provides a compelling example of how the three keys to profitability—sales, GP%, and

Expenses—interact to drive success.

The Current Situation

Celia has built a loyal client base thanks to her commitment to quality and excellent client service. Her monthly sales had plateaued, and although she was content with her profits, she knew there was potential for more. Through her local chamber of commerce, Celia connected with a shop owner in another city who was impressed by her products and eager to become an agent. This opportunity excited Celia, but the agent requested a 40% discount on her retail price to ensure profitability for their own business.

To decide whether the partnership made financial sense, Celia calculated the impact of the discount on her GP%.

Calculating the Adjusted GP%

Celia's GP% prior to the discount was 60%, calculated as follows:

Gross Profit = Selling Price – COGS

Gross Profit % = Gross Profit / Selling Price

At a retail price of $100, COGS is $40, and the GP is $60 or 60%.

With the proposed 40% discount, the new selling price would drop to $60. Celia recalculated her GP%:

Adjusted Gross Profit = Selling Price – COGS

= 60 – 40 = $20

Adjusted Gross Profit % = Adjusted Gross Profit / Selling Price

= 20 / 60 = 33.3%

This meant that for sales to the agent, her GP% would decrease from 60% to 33.3%.

Assessing the Opportunity

Despite the lower GP%, Celia realized that the arrangement still worked in her favor. Every sale to the agent would contribute to her gross profit. Since the agent agreed to cover shipping costs, these sales wouldn't add to her operating expenses. Additionally, any increase in total gross profit would flow directly to her net profit.

Confident in her calculations, Celia decided to go ahead with the agreement. She knew this expansion could help her reach new clients without incurring significant risks or costs.

Expansion Plan and Results

Over the next six months, the agent's sales grew steadily, reaching $12,000 per month. Celia's total sales increased to $52,000 per month, comprising $40,000 from her local shop and online store and $12,000 from the agent. Here's how her numbers looked:

Local Sales: $40,000 at a GP% of 60% = $24,000 GP

Agent Sales: $12,000 at a GP% of 33.3% = $3,996 GP

Total Gross Profit = $24,000 + $3,996 = $27,996

Average GP% = Total Gross Profit / Total Sales = 27,996 / 52,000 ≈ 53.8%[1]

Celia's gross profit increased by $3,996, which directly improved

---

1. You can test the accuracy of this statement by using the Excel spreadsheet called Gross profit, markup, and breakeven. Please refer to Appendix B: Resources.

her net profit by the same amount since her expenses remained unchanged.

Leveraging Increased Sales Volume

The growth in sales volume provided Celia with added leverage. She negotiated better pricing for her shipping materials, reducing her operating expenses. This small but significant adjustment further improved her net profit. The total improvement now amounted to more than $4,000 per month, proving how cost management can amplify the impact of sales growth.

Planning Ahead

Celia is always thinking a step ahead, and her next strategic move is to pursue natural certification for her product line. Her soaps and lotions already have a solid and loyal following thanks to their consistent quality and natural formulations. However, Celia believes that adding an official certification to her product labels will set her apart in the competitive marketplace. The certification will provide an additional layer of trust for her clients and elevate her products into a premium category.

Obtaining this certification is no small feat. It is a lengthy and costly process involving detailed documentation, testing, and compliance with rigorous standards. Despite the expense, Celia is confident in the value it will bring. Once certified, her products will justify higher pricing, directly enhancing both her revenue and GP%.

Celia has calculated that the cost of certification, while significant, is a one-time expense that can be written off. Renewal fees in subsequent years will also be manageable and classified as operating expenses. Her financial analysis shows that the expected improvement in gross profit will far exceed these additional costs, making the certification a sound investment.

This forward-thinking approach demonstrates Celia's understanding of how strategic decisions can drive profitability. By planning for the long term, she is positioning her business to maintain its competitive edge while increasing its financial resilience.

Key Lessons

Celia's success highlights the importance of understanding the interplay between the three keys to profitability:

Sales: Expanding into a new market increased her total sales by 30%.

Gross Profit Percentage (GP%): While the GP% decreased on agent sales, it was a calculated decision, and the overall increase in gross profit compensated for this trade-off.

Expenses: Reducing shipping material costs further boosted her net profit.

Celia's strategic approach enabled her to grow her business without taking on more risks, such as expanding her physical shop or introducing new product lines. By leveraging her strengths and making data-driven decisions, she achieved sustainable growth while maintaining operational stability.

Conclusion

This case study demonstrates how thoughtful decisions can balance the three keys to profitability. While improving all three simultaneously is ideal, Celia's story shows that prioritizing sales growth and expense reduction can lead to significant gains, even when GP% decreases. Her journey serves as an inspiring example of how strategic planning and careful analysis can unlock new opportunities for success.

Case Study 2: George's Poolside Profitability

Introduction

George owns a successful swimming pool construction business on the US West Coast. Over five years, he has built a compelling reputation for quality and reliability. The first two years were a learning curve, where George refined his processes, experimented with costing and pricing, and endured staff turnover until he found the right team. He also invested in essential equipment to create an efficient and profitable business.

Now, the business operates at its maximum capacity, delivering five pools per month. While George could increase capacity by adding labor and investing in more equipment, the associated capital expenditure (CapEx) and workforce expansion deterred him. Instead, George turned to the three keys to profitability—sales, GP%, and Expenses—to enhance his net profit without increasing capacity.

Sales: Adding Premium Features

George's business was already profitable, but he wanted to increase revenue without taking on more projects. He sought feedback from his past clients, who were highly satisfied with his work. Many expressed interest in modern coping tiles and higher-quality paving bricks for their pools—features that George hadn't offered before.

Recognizing the opportunity, George sourced these premium materials, which cost more but were in high demand. Confident in his company's formidable reputation, he decided to switch entirely to these high-quality options. To reflect the value of the upgrade, George raised his selling price by 9%.

Updated Sales Figures

At $60,000 per pool before the price increase, George's revenue from five pools was $300,000 per month. With the 9% price increase, the selling price per pool rose to $65,400. At full capacity, his monthly revenue increased to:

Total Sales = $65,400 × 5 pools = $327,000

This represented a $27,000 increase in revenue without increasing sales volume.

GP%: Reducing COGS Through Innovation

George's simplified costing system categorized all materials as part of the cost of goods sold (COGS), while labor and other operational costs were considered operating expenses. Over the past two years, his GP% stabilized at approximately 40%. The introduction of premium materials initially appeared to increase COGS and decrease GP%, but George didn't stop there.

He reviewed every component of his COGS, searching for ways to maintain or reduce costs without sacrificing quality. During a consultation with a potential client, George had a breakthrough. The client, a family with four children, expressed frustration with the traditional 6-foot depth of the deep end, which made it difficult to stand or play water games. George innovated a new pool floor design that reduced the deep-end depth to 4.5 feet, with a deeper center resembling a saucer. The design allowed adults and teenagers to stand comfortably while engaging in games and significantly reduced the amount of steel and concrete needed for construction.

Despite the added cost of premium coping and paving tiles, the new pool design reduced overall COGS. This innovative approach allowed George to increase his GP% while offering a superior product.

Updated GP% Figures

At $65,400 per pool and reduced COGS, George's new GP% improved. For simplicity:

COGS per pool dropped from $36,000 to $34,800

Gross Profit per pool = $65,400 - $34,800 = $30,600

GP% = $30,600 / $65,400 = 46.7%

Expenses: Eliminating Idle Time

George already ran a tight operation with well-managed expenses. His workforce consisted of five teams working in an assembly-line system, where each team specialized in specific tasks.

However, George noticed that there were idle days when one or more teams had no work due to the sequential nature of the system.

To address this inefficiency, George invested in cross-training his employees. Cross-training enabled team members to shift between tasks, cutting idle days and reducing payroll expenses. By streamlining his workforce, George reduced his overall labor costs while maintaining productivity.

Updated Expense Figures

George's payroll expenses decreased by 3.5%, contributing directly to an increase in net profit.

Net Effect

George's strategic adjustments in sales, GP%, and expenses worked together to enhance his profitability significantly. Here's the updated financial snapshot:

Total Sales = $327,000 (up from $300,000)

COGS = $34,800 per pool × 5 pools = $174,000 (down from $180,000)

Gross Profit = $327,000 - $174,000 = $153,000 (up from $120,000)

GP% = $153,000 / $327,000 ≈ 46.7% (up from 40%)

Operating Expenses decreased by 3.5%, further boosting net profit.

Key Lessons

Quality Can Demand a Premium Price: By introducing premium materials, George showed that clients are willing to pay more for higher quality. This strategy not only increased revenue but also enhanced his brand's reputation.

Sales Volume Isn't Everything: George proved that the same volume of sales could generate significantly higher revenue and profit when approached strategically.

Listen to Your Clients: Client feedback revealed valuable insights into their preferences and needs. The new pool design emerged directly from a client's suggestion, benefiting the business and increasing client satisfaction.

Never Stop Innovating: George's innovative floor design reduced COGS while improving the product's appeal. This breakthrough exemplifies the importance of continually searching for better ways to operate.

Conclusion

George's approach to enhancing profitability proves the power of focusing on the three keys: Sales, GP%, and Expenses. By raising prices, innovating to reduce production material, and streamlining expenses, he achieved substantial financial growth without increasing capacity. His story is a testament to the value of strategic thinking and innovation in driving business success.

Case Study 3: Dave's Landscaping Services

Introduction

Dave runs a small but reputable landscaping business in the West Midlands region of England. Over the past five years, he has developed a loyal client base by providing quality services, including fencing, patio and deck construction, garden structures, and garden scaping. Dave is well-regarded for his personalized service, keen attention to detail, and the reliability of his work.

However, driven by a desire to grow his business and boost profitability, Dave embarked on a series of strategic changes that he hoped would transform his operations. Unfortunately, his mismanagement of the three keys to profitability—sales, GP%, and Expenses—almost derailed his business. This case study explores the missteps Dave made, their consequences, and the lessons they offer.

Sales: Overextending Without Planning

Dave's first mistake was overreaching in his sales strategy. While his business thrived on residential projects, he decided to bid for commercial landscaping contracts to increase sales volume. He believed these contracts would bring in a steady income and help his business expand.

To secure these contracts, Dave underbid his competitors, offering prices barely above his costs. He reasoned that winning these projects would establish his name in the commercial sector and lead to more lucrative deals later. However, he needed to fully understand how devastating those low-profit margins would be for his business.

Compounding this issue, Dave overlooked the importance of requiring cash deposits prior to starting work. For his residential projects, it was standard practice to request an upfront payment to cover initial material costs. However, his commercial clients balked at the idea, and Dave, eager to win the contracts, agreed to commence work without deposits.

This decision placed a severe strain on his cash flow, as the larger scale of the commercial projects required significant outlays for materials and labor before any payment was received. Deposits could have mitigated this by ensuring immediate funds to support project expenses, reducing the risk of financial instability.

The commercial projects quickly consumed his team's time and resources, leaving little capacity to handle residential jobs. Delays became frequent, frustrating his loyal residential clients.

Negative reviews started appearing online, criticizing his tardiness and lack of attention to smaller projects. The very client base that had built his reputation began to dwindle.

GP%: Cutting Corners on Materials

As the commercial contracts stretched his budget, Dave looked to reduce costs by switching to cheaper materials. For example, he replaced premium treated timber with a budget option for fencing projects and used lower-grade patio stones for hardscaping.

Initially, this move seemed to help his margins, but the consequences were swift and damaging. Clients began noticing the reduced quality of his work. Within months, fences warped and splintered, while patios developed cracks and discoloration.

Warranty claims piled up, requiring repairs and replacements that eroded the little profit he had made on these projects.

Dave's reputation for quality, once his greatest strength, was now at risk. Word-of-mouth referrals, which had been a significant source of new residential business, slowed dramatically. Prospective clients hesitated to hire him, and his core market began shrinking.

Expenses: Misjudged Investments and Poor Management

Dave's eagerness to handle commercial contracts led him to make significant investments without accurately assessing their return on investment (ROI). He purchased expensive new equipment, such as a mini-excavator and a skid steer loader, to meet the expected demands of larger projects. While the equipment was necessary for commercial jobs, it often sat idle during slower months, tying up capital and creating cash flow problems.

To cope with the increased workload, Dave also hired more staff. However, he needed to integrate these workers more effectively into his existing team. The new hires lacked proper training, and the absence of streamlined processes created inefficiencies. For instance, crews often arrived at job sites without the required tools or clear instructions, causing delays and frustration.

The lack of team cohesion disrupted operations and led to unnecessary overtime, further inflating payroll expenses. What had been a tightly run operation now struggled with mismanagement and wasted resources.

Key Outcomes

Overextension Led to Delays and Lost Clients

Dave's focus on commercial contracts over his core residential market stretched his resources thin. The delays and declining quality of residential projects alienated loyal clients, leading to negative reviews and a shrinking client base.

Lower Margins and Rising Costs

The commercial contracts, with their slim profit margins, left little room for error. When warranty claims and added labor costs arose, they completely wiped out the gains from these projects.

Team Disruption

Dave's core team of workers had been efficient and dependable, but the hasty addition of inexperienced staff disrupted their workflow. The resulting inefficiencies created tension among employees and increased labor costs.

Reputation Damage

The combination of lower-quality materials, missed deadlines, and negative word-of-mouth severely harmed Dave's reputation. While he had once been known for quality and reliability, he now struggled to maintain trust in his brand.

Lessons from Dave's Story

Understand Your Client Base

Dave's core residential clients value quality and personalized service. By shifting his focus to commercial contracts, he neglected the very market that had built his business. Businesses should prioritize retaining and satisfying their core clients before trying to expand into new markets.

Never Compromise Quality

Dave's decision to use cheaper materials backfired, leading to dissatisfied clients and costly repairs. Short-term savings on materials can erode long-term profitability and harm a company's reputation.

Plan for Growth Strategically

Significant investments, like new equipment or added staff, should align with clear business goals and be supported by a solid ROI analysis. Dave's failure to assess these factors left him with underutilized assets and strained cash flow.

Balance Sales and Profit Margins

Increased sales volume doesn't always translate into higher profits. The slim margins on Dave's commercial contracts were unsustainable, especially when coupled with warranty claims and delays. It's critical to prioritize high-margin projects that contribute positively to the bottom line.

Turning the Corner

Recognizing the damage caused by his decisions, Dave began taking corrective action. He refocused his efforts on residential clients, leveraging his remaining loyal clients to rebuild his reputation.

He switched back to high-quality materials and made a point of personally inspecting each project for quality assurance.

To address inefficiencies, Dave implemented better team management practices. He cross-trained his staff to improve flexibility and reduce downtime. He also created standardized workflows to ensure teams arrived at job sites fully prepared.

Lastly, Dave sold some of the underutilized equipment, freeing up capital to stabilize his cash flow. By focusing on profitability rather than growth at any cost, Dave gradually restored his business's financial health and reputation.

Conclusion

Dave's story is a cautionary tale about the dangers of mismanaging the three keys to profitability. His well-intentioned efforts to grow his business nearly led to its collapse, but his willingness to learn from his mistakes allowed him to recover. This case study illustrates the importance of strategic planning, quality assurance, and a deep understanding of your market. By focusing on these principles, businesses can achieve sustainable growth and avoid the pitfalls that come with poorly executed expansions.

Chapter Recap

In this chapter, we explored three diverse case studies that illustrate the importance of managing the three keys to profitability. These real-world scenarios highlight both the potential for success and the risks of mismanagement, offering valuable lessons for business owners.

Celia's natural body care business demonstrates how calculated risks and innovation can fuel growth. By leveraging agent sales, renegotiating costs, and maintaining quality, she increased revenue and profitability without expanding her physical operations. Her forward-thinking approach, including plans for natural certification, underscores the value of strategic planning and client trust.

George's pool construction business exemplifies the rewards of aligning customer feedback with operational efficiency. By introducing premium features and innovating pool designs, he not only enhanced customer satisfaction but also increased gross profit margins. His success highlights the importance of focusing on high-margin projects and refining processes to maximize profitability.

In contrast, Dave's landscaping business provides a cautionary tale. His missteps—underbidding commercial contracts, using lower-quality materials, and poorly managing expenses—led to cash flow issues, strained resources, and a damaged reputation. Dave's story serves as a reminder that rapid growth without careful planning can destabilize even a strong business.

These case studies collectively emphasize that success lies in balancing the three keys. Whether it's improving revenue, maintaining quality, or controlling costs, thoughtful strategies and data-driven decisions are essential for achieving sustainable growth while avoiding common pitfalls.

Action Plan

Translate Lessons into Actionable Steps: Each insight should lead to clear, actionable strategies:

Sales: Focus on high-margin projects, leverage customer feedback, and consider the financial impact of pricing decisions.

GP%: Invest in quality and innovation to enhance value while managing costs.

Expenses: Regularly review and streamline operations to avoid inefficiencies and cash flow strain.

Customize for Your Business Context: Adapt the steps based on your industry, client base, and resources.

Chapter 8
The Simple Path to Profitability

"Focus on value creation, and profits will take care of themselves" – Jim Collins

Recap of the 3 Keys – Core Lessons from the Book

Throughout *3 Keys to Maximize Profitability*, we have focused on three essential levers: Sales, Gross Profit % (GP%), and Expenses. These elements are more than financial metrics; they are strategic tools that small business owners can use to unlock sustainable growth. This chapter summarizes the key lessons learned and provides a clear, actionable framework to maintain profitability.

Sales: The Engine of Growth

Sales are the lifeblood of any business. Increasing sales volume or revenue is often the most visible route to profitability. However, this book emphasizes that not all sales are created equal. Sustainable growth comes from building solid relationships with clients, not just clients. Clients are loyal, trust your brand, and return repeatedly.

Key lessons in sales growth include the importance of understanding your target market and tailoring your strategies to meet their needs. Branding, pricing, and client retention are vital components of this process. Effective branding builds trust and sets your business apart, while thoughtful pricing ensures you maximize revenue without alienating clients. Retaining clients costs less than acquiring new ones, making it a cornerstone of long-term success.

We also discussed leveraging routes to market and sales channels. Whether selling directly, through agents, or online platforms, choosing the right channel can maximize your reach and profitability. Combining these strategies creates a solid foundation for sustainable sales growth.

Gross Profit: The Measure of Operational Efficiency

Gross profit reflects the efficiency of your core operations. It highlights the profitability of your products or services before deducting operating expenses. Understanding GP helps you identify the value each sale contributes to the business.

Improving the GP% requires controlling the Cost of Goods Sold (COGS) while maintaining quality. Small adjustments, like negotiating supplier contracts or reducing waste, can lead to significant improvements. This chapter outlined how pricing strategies directly affect GP. By calculating markup and understanding the interplay between pricing and volume, you can find the sweet spot for maximizing the GP%.

In service industries, GP focuses on labor efficiency and direct material costs. For retailers and manufacturers, it revolves around production and inventory control. Regardless of the industry, focusing on GP ensures your business thrives operationally.

Expenses: The Driver of Profitability

Every dollar saved in expenses contributes directly to net profit. Managing expenses is not about slashing costs indiscriminately; it's about making strategic choices. Fixed expenses, like rent or salaries, provide stability but must be aligned with revenue.

Variable expenses, such as commissions or marketing, offer flexibility and should be optimized.

We explored strategies for managing both fixed and variable costs. These included automating tasks, outsourcing non-core activities, and negotiating better terms with suppliers. The break-even analysis highlighted the importance of balancing expenses with revenue. Knowing your break-even point allows you to make informed decisions and maintain control over cash flow.

Integration: The Power of the Three Keys

The true strength of these three keys lies in their integration. Changes in one area affect the others, creating a compounding effect. For example, higher sales at a better GP% and lower expenses result in exponential profitability.

This synergy is where small improvements across all three keys can deliver transformative results.

Focusing on the three keys—sales, GP, and expenses—simplifies your financial strategy. You no longer need to manage endless variables; instead, you direct your energy toward the areas that matter most. This simplicity is the heart of the book's message: profitability is not about complexity but clarity and focus.

In Summary

Profitability is achievable for any business that applies these principles with consistency and discipline. By mastering the three keys, small business owners can secure financial stability, enable growth, and achieve long-term success.

This framework is your roadmap to turning challenges into opportunities and aspirations into achievements.

Encouragement to Take Action

Profitability might seem like an intimidating goal, but it starts with simple, deliberate steps. This book has armed you with a practical framework, focusing on three keys: Sales, Gross Profit, and Expenses. Now, it's time to act. No business transforms overnight, but every small step you take will build momentum.

Start Small, Think Big

The path to profitability begins with small, manageable changes. Break your goals into actionable tasks. Simplify your focus. Instead of trying to fix everything at once, start by improving one key area. For example, revisit your sales strategy. Are you effectively connecting with your target market? Could your branding or pricing align better with your goals?

These adjustments may seem minor at first. However, even small improvements can lead to meaningful results over time. The key is consistency. Like a snowball rolling downhill, small efforts compound. Over weeks and months, these steps gain momentum, driving significant growth and profitability.

Progress Is More Important Than Perfection

As a business owner, it's easy to get caught up in trying to perfect every detail. Remember, progress matters more than perfection. You don't need to overhaul your entire business to see results. Start by implementing just one idea from this book. Evaluate it. Measure the outcome. Then, refine and scale your efforts.

Mistakes are inevitable. You'll learn more from trying and adjusting than from waiting to get everything right. Every decision you make teaches you something valuable. The lessons you learn along the way will make you a stronger, more confident entrepreneur.

Focus on What You Can Control

Business can be unpredictable. Economic changes, market trends, or unexpected challenges might seem overwhelming. But while you can't control everything, you can focus on what matters most: sales, gross profit, and expenses.

Ask yourself, "What can I improve today?" Maybe it's streamlining an expense or negotiating better supplier terms. Perhaps it's designing a client retention program or adjusting your pricing. These are actions within your control. Focus on them. With time, the results will speak for themselves.

Simplifying your priorities also helps manage stress. You don't need to solve every problem at once. By narrowing your efforts, you free up energy to make meaningful progress where it counts.

Celebrate Small Wins

Every milestone deserves recognition. Did you successfully renegotiate with a supplier? Celebrate that win. Did you boost your gross profit by even one percent? That's a step toward your larger goal. Acknowledging these moments builds confidence and motivation.

Success is a journey, not a destination. By celebrating small victories, you stay motivated and focused. Over time, these small wins add up, moving you closer to financial stability and growth.

Build a Habit of Simplicity

The lessons in this book emphasize clarity and simplicity. Overcomplicating your strategies can lead to confusion and wasted effort. Instead, focus on the fundamentals. This doesn't mean avoiding innovation or growth, but it does mean ensuring your foundation is solid.

A simple habit like reviewing your income statement monthly can provide powerful insights. Monitoring your sales trends or calculating your GP percentage regularly equips you to make smarter, faster decisions. These habits keep you connected to your business's performance and help you act proactively.

You're Not Alone

Running a business can feel isolated, but you're not alone. Many entrepreneurs face the same challenges, doubts, and fears. The key to overcoming them is perseverance. Remember, every successful business owner started somewhere. They faced obstacles and made mistakes, but they kept going.

Surround yourself with support. Connect with mentors, join business networks, or seek advice from professionals. Learning from others not only accelerates your progress but also reassures you that your challenges are shared and solvable.

Take the First Step

You've completed this book. Now, the next step is yours. Start with one small action. Revisit your goals for sales, GP%, or expenses. Commit to improving just one metric. Once you've taken that first step, the next one becomes more effortless.

The path to profitability doesn't require grand gestures. It requires consistent, focused effort. By applying what you've learned and staying persistent, you'll build a profitable, resilient business.

The journey starts now. Trust in your ability to grow, adapt, and thrive. Your business's best days are ahead, waiting for you to act.

Looking Ahead

As your business achieves profitability, new opportunities will arise. With a solid foundation built on the three keys, you're equipped to face challenges and embrace growth. This closing section explores areas to consider as your business evolves.

Scaling for Growth

Profitability creates room to scale your business. Scaling involves expanding operations, increasing capacity, or entering new markets. It requires careful planning to ensure that growth doesn't outpace your resources. Look at your systems and processes. Are they prepared to handle higher volumes of sales or production?

Strategic scaling means balancing growth with operational efficiency. Avoid the temptation to grow too quickly without maintaining quality. Leverage what you've learned about expense control and gross profit to guide sustainable expansion.

Diversifying Revenue Streams

Relying on a single product, service, or client base limits your growth potential. Consider diversifying. This could mean introducing complementary products, entering a new market, or offering value-added services. Diversification spreads risk and creates new revenue opportunities.

Before diversifying, evaluate the costs and benefits. Ensure that new ventures align with your brand and target market. Diversification is most effective when built on your existing strengths.

Investing in Technology

As businesses grow, technology plays a critical role in driving efficiency. Tools for customer relationship management (CRM), inventory tracking, and financial analysis can simplify operations and improve decision-making. Automation reduces repetitive tasks, allowing you to focus on strategy and innovation.

Consider adopting accounting software with advanced features, such as forecasting and real-time reporting. Technology investments should align with your business needs and deliver measurable returns.

Developing Leadership

Growth requires more than systems and technology; it demands strong leadership. As a business owner, your role may evolve from hands-on management to guiding strategy. Developing leadership skills helps you inspire your team and maintain focus on long-term goals.

Empower others in your organization by delegating responsibilities. A team that feels trusted and valued will contribute to your business's success. Leadership isn't just about directing—it's about building a culture of accountability, innovation, and shared purpose.

Staying Agile

The business landscape constantly changes. Competitors, market trends, and economic shifts can challenge even the most profitable companies. Agility is your ability to adapt and innovate in response to change.

Regularly assess your business's performance. Revisit your income statement and track key metrics. Stay informed about industry developments and be prepared to pivot when necessary. Agility allows you to seize opportunities while navigating uncertainties.

Conclusion

Looking ahead, your journey doesn't end with profitability—it begins there. Scaling, diversification, technology, leadership, and agility are your next steps. By applying the lessons from this book and staying focused, you'll continue to grow, thrive, and achieve new milestones.

Afterword

Thank you for reading!

If you found this book helpful, I'd greatly appreciate it if you could take a moment to leave a review on Amazon. Your feedback not only helps me improve but also assists other readers in finding the right resources. Scan the QR code (or click on it) to share your thoughts.

I appreciate your support!

Appendix A: Action Plan

All resources can be downloaded from our website, visit www.impisimedia.com/resources. You'll need to register for a free account and enter the access code to unlock the materials. **Access Code: SBPRO**

Combining the various chapters' plans, you can use this plan to help you plot your way.

Unlocking Sales Growth

Identify Your Target Market: Define your ideal client by analyzing demographics, buying behaviors, and needs. This step helps you create tailored messages and strategies to engage the right audience effectively.

Segment Your Client Base: Divide your target market into smaller groups with shared characteristics. Use this segmentation to personalize your marketing efforts, making them more relevant and impactful.

Refine Your Brand Identity: Ensure that your branding aligns with your market positioning. Consistently communicate your brand values and voice across all platforms to build trust and recognition.

Choose the Best Routes to Market: Select strategic pathways to deliver your product or service to clients. Consider direct sales, partnerships, or online channels based on client preferences and your brand's goals.

Set a Competitive Pricing Strategy: Choose a pricing model that reflects value without compromising profit. Avoid lowering prices unnecessarily; instead, emphasize quality and uniqueness to attract clients.

Focus on Client Retention: Implement retention strategies like loyalty programs, personalized service, and consistent communication to build lasting client relationships.

Mastering Gross Profit

To improve the Gross Profit Percentage (GP%), small business owners should start by assessing their current Cost of Goods Sold (COGS) structure.

Begin with a detailed breakdown of COGS, identifying all cost elements and their impact on profitability.

Set a GP% target that aligns with your business goals and industry standards. Once you have clarity on your baseline and goals, prioritize areas for improvement.

Focus on incremental, sustainable changes rather than one-time cost-cutting. Implement as many of the 18 approaches discussed in the chapter.

Make it a point to regularly review pricing and discount strategies, and align them with your desired GP%, adapting them as your business and market conditions change.

Finally, track your progress with regular GP% evaluations. Small adjustments over time will compound, creating a stronger, more profitable foundation for your business.

Managing Expenses

Understand Your Expenses: Differentiate between fixed and variable expenses. Track each carefully to know where your money is going and how costs fluctuate with sales.

Use Breakeven Analysis: Calculate your breakeven point to know the minimum sales required to cover expenses. Regularly test scenarios using the provided Excel model to see how changes in expenses or sales impact profitability.

Control Costs: Implement the strategies and tactics for reducing expenses discussed in this chapter.

Leverage Technology: Investigate automation options for repetitive tasks and explore AI tools for insights that can enhance efficiency.

Balance Investments with Expense Reduction: Prioritize high-ROI investments and maintain strict control over operational expenses, especially during uncertain periods.

Integrating the Three Keys

Engage Your Team: Involve team members directly in goal-setting and problem-solving. For example, include production staff in discussions about GP% improvements and administrative teams in expense reviews.

Set Targeted Goals: Define specific, realistic targets for each key—Sales, GP%, and Expenses. Use the SMART principle (Specific,

Measurable, Achievable, Relevant, Time-bound).

Establish Monthly Reviews: Schedule monthly reviews to check progress on each key. This frequency allows you to catch trends early.

Act Quickly on Deviations: When performance slips, analyze the cause and respond promptly with focused actions.

Pursue Continuous Improvement: Treat every review as a chance to refine your strategies. Even when goals are met, seek new efficiencies or opportunities for growth.

Implement Financial Planning

Understand Your Profit Metrics: Focus on Net Profit, Operating Profit, and EBITDA to assess profitability. Use Net Profit as your primary indicator but understand how the other metrics provide additional insights.

Leverage Financial Statements: Review the income statement and balance sheet regularly (monthly). Use graphs and trendlines to track changes in sales, GP, GP%, and expenses over time.

Manage Cash Flow Actively: Monitor inflows from cash and credit sales and maintain clear debtor terms. Avoid cash shortages by managing inventory, optimizing payment terms, and using credit wisely when needed.

Combine Forecasting, Budgeting, and Cash Flow: Develop a 3-in-1 document that integrates forecasting, budgeting, and cash flow projections. This tool provides a unified view of your finances, helping you adjust quickly to changes.

Lessons from Case Studies

Translate Lessons into Actionable Steps: Each insight should lead to clear, actionable strategies:

Sales: Focus on high-margin projects, leverage customer feedback, and consider the financial impact of pricing decisions.

GP%: Invest in quality and innovation to enhance value while managing costs.

Expenses: Regularly review and streamline operations to avoid inefficiencies and cash flow strain.

Customize for Your Business Context: Adapt the steps based on your industry, client base, and resources.

Appendix B: Resources

All resources can be downloaded from our website, visit www.impisimedia.com/resources. You'll need to register for a free account and enter the access code to unlock the materials. **Access Code: SBPRO**

Table of Resources

1. Brand strategy and positioning template
2. Hymn sheet link
3. Gross profit, markup and breakeven
4. Recommended reading

1. Brand Strategy and Positioning Template

1. Brand strategy

Here are five questions to ask yourself about your brand strategy.

1.1 Who is your ideal client?

Knowing your ideal client allows you to tailor your branding efforts to resonate with the right audience. This is the person who not only needs what you offer but is also aligned with your values and vision. Defining your audience helps ensure that your message speaks directly to those who are most likely to engage with your brand.

1.2 What is your ideal client's perception of your business?

Understanding how your clients perceive your brand is essential for shaping your strategy. Gathering feedback through surveys, informal conversations, or direct interviews can provide valuable insights. Since not all clients will voluntarily share their opinions, you may need to ask directly to gain the insights necessary to adjust your branding.

1.3 What is your clear and concise message?

In a crowded marketplace, your brand needs to stand out. Having a clear, concise message allows you to capture attention quickly. Imagine meeting your ideal client at a networking event. How would you explain what you do in 30 seconds? This "elevator pitch" should be applied consistently across all client interactions to reinforce your brand's message.

1.4 Do you have a proven process that converts attention into sales?

Once you've captured the attention of your ideal client, you need a strategy to guide them through the customer journey. Whether through email campaigns, targeted content, or personalized offers, having a system in place that nurtures leads will result in more conversions and stronger client relationships.

1.5 Are you tracking results and refining your strategy?

Many businesses do not monitor the effectiveness of their branding efforts. Implementing tracking measures such as dedicated landing pages or client surveys helps gather data on what's working and what isn't. This data allows you to refine your branding strategy, ensuring it evolves with the needs and perceptions of your clients.

2. Brand positioning

2.1 What is the clients' defining characteristic?

2.2 What is their enduring need?

These two questions help you clarify who your target clients are and what they consistently seek from your product or service. This insight allows you to create a focused and relevant brand message.

Explanation of the brand positioning exercise

[Name] is the brand of [core business] that [outcome of service] due to its [reason for outcome] because people who [defining characteristic] want [enduring need].

The brand positioning exercise is designed to help businesses clearly articulate their value proposition by identifying what makes their clients unique and what those clients desire in the long term. By filling in the blanks (bold letters) in the provided template, businesses can craft a concise and powerful statement that captures their core offering, the outcome of their services, and why it appeals to their target audience. This exercise simplifies the process of positioning your brand in a way that resonates with your clients, making your value and promise clear.

Example of brand positioning using the template

BreezeHomes is the brand of **eco-friendly real estate services** that **provides sustainable, energy-efficient homes** due to its **innovative use of green technology** because people who **care about the environment** want **homes that reduce their carbon**

footprint.

This positioning statement clarifies that BreezeHomes targets environmentally-conscious clients and fulfills their need for sustainability through its expertise in green technology.

2. Hymn Sheet

XYZ Company communications (hymn sheet template)

1. Market Environment and Core Problem

Guidance: Describe the current market landscape in which your business operates. Focus on the primary problem your target clients face, and how your company's offerings provide a solution. Keep it concise and focus on the relevance of the problem to your target audience.

2. Products and/or Services

Guidance: Provide a concise summary of the products or services your business offers. Focus on the essentials—what you sell. Detailed descriptions can follow later, in paragraph 10, so keep this high-level and easy to understand.

3. Unique Selling Point (USP)

Guidance: What sets your business apart from competitors? Describe your unique approach, innovation, or standout feature that makes your product or service different. Focus on the value that this uniqueness delivers to your clients.

4. Market Positioning (Elevator Pitch)

Guidance: This is your quick, memorable response to the question, "What do you do?" Prepare three versions of your elevator pitch:

- **Short** (10-15 words): For brief introductions.

- **Medium** (20-50 words): For when you have a little more time.

- **Long** (up to 75 words): For slightly more in-depth explanations. Keep it clear, concise, and focused on your value proposition.

5. Vision

Guidance: Your vision is aspirational—it is where the company ultimately wants to go, even if it may never be fully achieved. It should inspire and guide long-term direction. Keep it broad and motivating.

6. Mission

Guidance:
This explains what your company does every day to move toward the vision. It's your company's purpose in action. Focus on what your employees work toward daily and how that aligns with solving client problems or delivering value.

7. Core Values

Guidance: List 4 or 5 key values that guide your company's behavior and decision-making. For each value, include a brief explanation. Keep the descriptions practical, explaining how each value affects daily operations and the client experience.

8. Business Principles

Guidance: These are the guiding principles that influence your business decisions and actions. They should reflect your company's priorities and how you manage challenges, opportunities, and ethical considerations. Keep them actionable and clear.

9. Why Us?

Guidance: Explain why clients should choose you over your competition. Focus on your competitive advantages, such as better service, unique expertise, or a specific problem you solve that others do not. Be clear about the tangible value you offer.

10. Detailed Value Offering

Guidance: Here, you can expand on the product or service descriptions you provided earlier. Focus on the details of how your offerings solve client problems or improve their experience. Avoid getting too technical; instead, highlight the key benefits your clients care about most.

General Tips: Keep each section straightforward and easy to read. Aim for clarity over complexity and ensure that the language resonates with both internal teams and external stakeholders. This template should serve as a quick reference point that helps everyone "sing from the same hymn sheet."

EXAMPLE: ABC Company communications

1. Market Environment and Core Problem

Small and medium-sized businesses often struggle with digital transformation. Many lack the technical ability to adopt cloud-based solutions that could boost efficiency and reduce costs. ABC Company addresses this gap by offering tailored digital solutions for businesses looking to modernize.

2. Products and/or Services

ABC Company provides cloud-based software solutions, IT consulting, and ongoing technical support. We specialize in implementing customizable platforms that help businesses improve their workflows and data management.

3. Unique Selling Point (USP)

Our unique approach combines comprehensive IT consulting with personalized cloud-based solutions. Unlike other providers, we focus on small to mid-sized businesses and offer customizable packages tailored to individual business needs.

4. Market Positioning (Elevator Pitch)

- Short: We help businesses streamline operations through personalized cloud-based solutions.

- Medium: ABC Company offers customizable cloud solutions and IT consulting to help small and medium-sized businesses improve efficiency and reduce costs.

- Long: ABC Company specializes in personalized cloud solutions for small and medium-sized businesses. We combine IT consulting with tailored software platforms that help companies manage their workflows more efficiently, cut costs, and stay ahead of competitors.

5. Vision

To empower every small and medium-sized business to achieve digital transformation and operate with the same efficiency as large corporations.

6. Mission

We provide customized cloud solutions and expert IT consulting to help businesses thrive in a digital world. Our mission is to simplify technology adoption for our clients, enabling them to focus on growing their core business.

7. Values

- **Innovation**: We embrace innovative technology to provide the best solutions for our clients.

- **Client-Centric**: Our client's success is our top priority, and we are committed to helping them achieve their goals.

- **Integrity**: We operate with transparency, honesty, and an intense sense of ethics.

- **Collaboration**: We believe in teamwork, both within our company and with our clients.

- **Excellence**: We strive for excellence in every solution we deliver.

8. Business Principles

- **Client Success**: We prioritize the long-term success of our clients by delivering solutions that align with their business goals, ensuring continuous support and innovation to help them grow.

- **Employee Empowerment**: We foster a culture of learning, collaboration, and growth within our team, ensuring that every employee feels valued and empowered to contribute to our shared success.

- **Community Engagement**: We actively take part in and give back to the communities in which we live and work, believing that strong, healthy communities are the foundation for sustainable business success.

- **Environmental Responsibility**: We are committed to minimizing our environmental footprint by adopting sustainable practices in our operations and encouraging our clients to do the same through eco-friendly digital solutions.

- **Innovation and Excellence**: We continuously seek new ways to improve our products and services, driving innovation and maintaining excellence in everything we do.

9. Why Us?

Clients choose ABC Company because we offer customized cloud solutions that meet the specific needs of small and medium-sized businesses. We provide ongoing IT support and ensure seamless integration of modern technologies. Our focus on personalized service, combined with our expertise in digital transformation, sets us apart from other providers.

10. Detailed Value Offering

At ABC Company, we deliver a range of cloud-based solutions that include data management, workflow automation, and secure IT infrastructure. Our expert consultants collaborate with each client to understand their unique challenges and design solutions that increase efficiency and reduce costs. We also provide ongoing support to ensure that clients maximize the value of their technology investments.

3. Gross Profit, Markup and Breakeven

A very versatile Excel spreadsheet created for you to calculate your Gross Profit, Markup and Breakeven. This file can be downloaded from our website, follow the download instructions at the beginning of this Appendix.

4. Recommended Reading

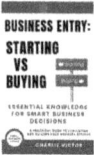

Small Business Series
Business Entry: Starting vs Buying

Smart Work-Life Series
The Wolf's Edge - Strategies for Intelligent Living

Appendix C: Glossary

These definitions are concise and intended for quick reference, rather than comprehensive explanations as found in formal investment or business finance dictionaries.

3-in-1 Financial Planning Document: A combined financial tool for small businesses that integrates forecasting, budgeting, and cash flow projections, offering a comprehensive view of financial health.

Absorption Costing: A costing method that includes all production-related expenses—direct materials, direct labor, and overhead—in the cost of goods sold.

Accrual Accounting: A method of accounting where transactions are recorded when revenue is earned or expenses are incurred, regardless of when cash is exchanged.

Acquisition: The process of attracting new clients to a business, often through marketing and outreach efforts.

Aging Report: A report that categorizes accounts receivable based on the length of time they have been outstanding, used to track overdue payments.

Average Gross Profit %: The overall gross profit percentage that reflects the contribution of different products or departments, based on their sales and respective gross profit percentages.

Brand Identity: The visible elements of a brand, such as logo, colors, and design, that help clients recognize and connect with the business.

Brand Positioning: The place a product or service occupies in the minds of clients relative to competitors, influenced by price, quality, and brand perception.

Brand Promise: A commitment made to clients regarding the experience and quality they can expect from a brand's product or service.

Branding: The creation and management of a brand's identity, values, and personality, helping it stand out in the market and build trust.

Breakeven Point: The sales level at which total revenue equals total expenses, resulting in no profit or loss.

Capital Expenditure (CapEx): Funds used by a business to acquire, upgrade, or maintain physical assets such as property, buildings, or equipment. CapEx is often used to expand or improve business operations.

Cash Flow Statement: A financial statement showing the cash inflows and outflows from operating, investing, and financing activities over a period, providing insight into liquidity.

Client Relationship Management (CRM): A system for managing interactions with clients to build long-term relationships and improve client satisfaction.

Client Retention: Strategies focused on keeping existing clients engaged and loyal to maximize lifetime value and reduce acquisition costs.

Client Segmentation: The process of dividing a target market into smaller, defined groups based on shared characteristics to tailor marketing efforts.

Compounding Effect: The phenomenon where improvements in multiple areas simultaneously produce an exponential increase in net profit rather than a simple additive effect.

Cost of Goods Sold (COGS): Direct costs associated with producing goods sold by a business, including materials and labor.

Cost of Services Sold (COSS): The direct costs involved in delivering a service, such as labor and materials.

Depreciation: The accounting process of allocating the cost of a tangible asset over its useful life. It represents a non-cash expense that does not directly affect cash flow.

EBIT (Earnings Before Interest and Taxes): A profitability metric that shows profit from core business operations by excluding interest and tax expenses.

EBITDA (Earnings Before Interest, Taxes, Depreciation, and Amortization): A profitability metric that indicates a business's core profitability by excluding financing and non-cash expenses.

EBITDA: Earnings Before Interest, Taxes, Depreciation, and Amortization. A financial metric that reflects a company's operating profitability by excluding the effects of financing and accounting decisions.

Exponential Growth: Growth that accelerates over time due to a multiplying effect from simultaneous improvements in more than one profitability key.

Fixed Expenses: Business costs that remain constant regardless of production or sales levels, such as rent, insurance, and salaries.

Forecasting: The process of estimating future revenue, costs, and profits based on historical data and trends, used for long-term planning.

Gross Profit (GP): The profit a business earns after deducting the cost of goods sold from sales revenue, indicating operational efficiency.

Gross Profit Percentage (GP%): The ratio of gross profit to sales, showing how much of each sales dollar remains after covering the cost of goods sold.

Income Statement: A financial statement summarizing a company's revenue, costs, and profit over a period, reflecting its financial performance.

Interest Expense: The cost incurred by a business on borrowed funds, such as loans or credit, usually calculated as a percentage of the principal amount.

Inventory Optimization: Managing stock levels to reduce holding costs, prevent obsolescence, and align with demand forecasts.

Just-in-Time (JIT) Inventory: An inventory management strategy aiming to reduce stock levels by timing orders closely with production needs to minimize holding costs.

Linear Growth: A steady, proportional increase in net profit that results from improving one key area (e.g., sales, GP%, or expenses) while the others remain constant.

Market Positioning: Strategically placing a brand or product in a specific market to make it distinct and desirable to the target audience.

Marketing Plan: A tactical document detailing the actions, timelines, and campaigns needed to achieve a marketing strategy.

Marketing Strategy: A high-level plan that outlines the overall approach to reaching the target market and achieving brand objectives.

Markup (MU): The amount added to the cost price of a product to determine its selling price.

Markup Percentage (MU%): The markup expressed as a percentage of the cost price, rather than the selling price.

Maximum Discount Percentage: The largest discount that can be applied to a product while covering the cost of goods sold and maintaining profitability.

Net Profit: The final profit after all expenses, including taxes and interest, have been deducted, representing the true profitability of the business.

Obsolescence: The reduction in value of stock due to technological advances, regulatory changes, or shifts in consumer preferences.

Operating Expense (OpEx): Day-to-day costs required to run a business, such as rent, utilities, and salaries, which are distinct from capital expenses.

Operating Profit: Also called EBIT, this metric reflects profit from core business activities, excluding interest and taxes, focusing on operational performance.

Outsourcing: Contracting out certain business processes to third-party providers, often to reduce expenses or improve efficiency in non-core areas.

Pilferage: The loss of stock due to employee theft, typically within a business setting, affecting inventory and profitability.

Pricing Power: The ability of a business to set prices above competitors' levels due to unique product differentiation or brand strength.

Pricing Strategy: Planned pricing models that reflect a product's value and target market, balancing affordability with profitability.

Product Differentiation: The process of distinguishing a product from competitors' products by emphasizing unique features, quality, or branding.

Profitability: The ability of a business to generate profit after covering costs, essential for long-term sustainability and growth.

Rolling Budget: A budgeting approach that continuously updates the budget by adding a new period (month or quarter) as each period ends.

Routes to Market: The strategic pathways a business uses to bring its products or services to clients, distinct from specific sales channels.

Sales Growth: An increase in sales revenue over a defined period, signaling business expansion and market traction.

Sales Mix: The distribution of total sales across various products or services, which can affect gross profit percentage.

Shoplifting: The act of stealing goods from a retail store by non-employees, affecting the cost of goods sold and profitability.

Simplified Costing: A method used by small manufacturers, focusing on direct materials while treating other costs as operating expenses.

Synergy: The combined effect of multiple strategies that produce a greater outcome together than the sum of their individual impacts.

Target Market: The specific group of clients most likely to benefit from and purchase a business's products or services.

Trendline: A visual tool on a graph that shows the general direction of data points over time, useful for identifying trends in financial performance.

Trickle Effect: A gradual increase in profitability that occurs as improvements in one key area influence and enhance performance in other areas over time.

Value-Added Services: Additional services or features provided to enhance the product's perceived value, allowing for higher pricing without significant cost increases.

Value-Based Pricing: A pricing strategy based on the perceived value of a product to the client rather than solely on cost or competition.

Variable Costing: A costing method that includes only variable costs, such as direct materials and direct labor, in the cost of goods sold, excluding fixed overhead.

Variable Expense Percentage (VE%): The ratio of variable expenses to sales, representing how much of each sales dollar goes toward variable costs.

Variable Expenses: Costs that fluctuate in direct proportion to production or sales volume, such as sales commissions, shipping, and marketing expenses.

Working Capital: The capital available for day-to-day operations, calculated as current assets minus current liabilities, indicating short-term financial health.

Appendix D: Supplemental Glossary

This supplement contains noteworthy words and concepts not used in the book.

These definitions are concise and intended for quick reference, rather than comprehensive explanations as found in formal investment or business finance dictionaries.

Sales-Related Terms

Sales volume: The total quantity of products or services sold.

Sales pipeline: A visual representation of the sales process, from leads to closed deals.

Sales quota: A specific sales target assigned to a salesperson or sales team.

Sales commission: A payment to a salesperson based on the number of sales they generate.

Revenue-Related Terms

Top line: Another term for revenue, often used in financial statements.

Revenue cycle: The process of generating revenue, from sales to collection.

Revenue per client: The average revenue generated by each client.

Revenue recognition: The accounting principles that govern when revenue is recorded.

Revenue model: The way a company generates revenue, such as subscriptions, advertising, or product sales.

Additional Concepts

Sales efficiency: A measure of how effectively a company converts sales efforts into revenue.

Client lifetime value: The total revenue a customer is expected to generate over their lifetime.

About the Author

Born in South Africa and now residing in Panama, Charlie Victor has dedicated his life to the world of small business. With a Bachelor of Commerce and a postgraduate degree in Investment Management, he has a solid academic foundation that complements his practical experience. A serial entrepreneur, Charlie has spent his entire career immersed in small business finance, development and management.

After serving as a pilot in the military, he turned his focus to the business world, assisting hundreds of small businesses in their growth journeys. Many of these ventures have flourished into large, profitable enterprises. Before taking early retirement, Charlie co-founded and served as COO of an international SME finance company where he played a pivotal role in establishing and training in-country teams.

With extensive travel experience, much of it work-related, Charlie draws on his extensive experiences to provide practical, actionable advice for prospective entrepreneurs and new small business owners.

About the Publisher

Impisi™ Media is a dynamic publishing company dedicated to creating and distributing high-quality intellectual property, including books, e-books, audiobooks, and journals.

Our content is crafted to inform, inspire, and empower a global audience. Our commitment to innovation and excellence drives us to deliver content that resonates and adds value to our readers and listeners.

Visit our website https://impisimedia.com

f facebook.com/impisimedia

⊙ instagram.com/impisimedia

𝓟 pinterest.com/impisimedia

www.ingramcontent.com/pod-product-compliance
Lightning Source LLC
Chambersburg PA
CBHW071602210326
41597CB00019B/3358